NOW

I'M A CHRISTIAN

● JIM SMITH

Scripture Union
130 City Road, London EC1V 2NJ

First published 1990
Reprinted 1991

ISBN 0 86201 546 4

Printed in Great Britain by Ebenezer Baylis & Son Ltd, Worcester and London.

Jim Who?

Jim Smith is an international evangelist associated with the Church Pastoral Aid Society. From 1990 his ministry is to be totally funded by The Servant Partnership – a group committed to support his prophetic and evangelistic work worldwide. He lives in County Durham with his wife Mary. They have four sons.

Acknowledgements

The North Eastern Council on Addictions (1 Mosely Street, Newcastle upon Tyne NE1 1YE) provided information for the section on drugs. NSPCC publications (67 Saffron Hill, London EC1) supplied information used in the section on abuse. The True Freedom Trust (PO Box 3, Upton, Wirral, Merseyside L49 6NY) provided information for the section on homosexuality. Information for the section on smoking came from the Health Education Authority (Mabledon Place, London WC1).

The Bible text in this publication is from the Good News Bible, published by the Bible Societies and Collins. Old Testament: © American Bible Society 1979. New Testament:© American Bible Society 1966, 1971, 1976. Used by permission.

Contents

Start here!

Don't *read* 'Now I'm a Christian', because it's not that kind of book! To get the best from it, use it like a box of chocolates – dip in and take the ones you like the best! Look through the contents list, pick out the subjects that seem most important to you today, look at them, and leave the rest for another day. Each topic has practical suggestions, as well as things to think and pray about.

There are four main sections. 'Faith' tells you how to get to know Jesus for yourself, and how to stay close to him. 'Lifestyle' tells you how he expects you to live. 'Issues' looks at some things in the world around us which Christians have to think through, and 'Sharing' will help you to tell others about Jesus.

This book won't just give you some answers, it will pose lots of questions, too. Many of us find that trying to answer questions on our own is difficult. That's why discussing things in groups is so useful. Sometimes, other people can see things that we can't, and we see things that others can't. So together, as we get stuck into a question, we can find the answer.

• Do you belong to a group of Christians? Then why not suggest to your leader that the group might tackle some of the issues in this book? Don't hesitate – leaders like to have suggestions from their group.

• Do you meet with a couple of friends? Then why not work through some of the questions together, and if you get stuck, ask for some help from someone who knows a bit more about Christian things than you do.

• Do you have a school Christian Union? Then why not do some of the questions together, as a group?

Remember, no matter how hard it is to get a group going, it's always worth it. Most of us find groups a help.

Now I'm a Christian is a good book to have beside your bed, along with your Bible. Not only will it help you, but it will help you help your friends to find Jesus as well.

Knowing JESUS for YOURSELF

LINK: What do I believe about Jesus? (page 18)
The Holy Spirit (page 8)

During the 1960s an event took place in China called the cultural revolution. Millions of Chinese people suffered terribly during this dreadful period, and many people who believed in Jesus Christ were humiliated, persecuted, tortured and killed. Some were made to kneel in the gutters to be mocked and spat on, and some had their heads shaved, leaving their hair in the shape of a cross as a mark of shame. In one town, the ministers were made to walk the streets with dunce's hats on, a woman was beaten to death, and then twenty Christians were made to kneel in front of a burning pile of books until they suffered severe burns – a large crowd looked on. This was not uncommon.

If people can stand this sort of treatment for the Christian faith then we ought to take a look at what they believe. What are the basics of Christian faith?

1 Something is wrong

Read these verses:

"I have come in order that you might have life – life in all its fullness" (John 10:10).

Ask yourself

● Is your life full? Do you feel satisfied?
● Do you feel lost, empty, bored, frustrated, afraid?

God intended that we should feel fullness, not emptiness, but many people do feel empty, wasted and alone. The Bible makes it clear to us why this is:

"Suppose one of you has a hundred sheep and loses one of them – what does he do? He leaves the other ninety-nine sheep in the pasture and goes looking for the one that got lost

until he finds it. When he finds it, he is so happy that he puts it on his shoulders and carries it back home. Then he calls his friends and neighbours together and says to them, 'I am so happy I found my lost sheep. Let us celebrate!' In the same way, I tell you, there will be more joy in heaven over one sinner who repents than over ninety-nine respectable people who do not need to repent" (Luke 15:4–7).

We don't live satisfied lives because, like the one sheep, we have got separated from God. THINK: Have you become separated from God? Did you:
● just not know that he was there?
● just not care if he was there?
● drift away from him?
● reject him?

Either way, the truth remains the same – it's possible to get lost and cut off from God. That's why life isn't full. That's why you feel that there must be more to it.

2 God doesn't want us lost

It isn't God's will that we should be lost, and far from his loving and powerful presence. The Bible tells us that God wants everybody to be saved (which means having the separation between us and God ended, so we're close to him again). That includes you, no matter how far you feel from him right now. Like the shepherd, God has come looking for you, because he wants you back home.

THINK: What do you think you are worth as a person? God thinks you're worth as much as his Son Jesus! Read on.

3 God has done something

Read Luke 23. This is the story of the last weeks of Jesus' life, his arrest, trial and death. Why did he go through all this? The answer starts with our problem – we are lost, separated from God by the things we do and say which hurt others, damage us and hurt God. It's as though there is a huge gap between us and God, and although we try to bridge the gap, it just can't be done. Trying to be good, going to church, even saying our prayers can't get us across. As the prophet Isaiah said, 'It is your sins that separate you from God' (Isaiah 59:2). There's nothing we can do about it.

Jesus suffered because he loved us (John 3:16). By his death he paid the price for all our wrong. His cross has made a bridge for us.

Read this:

"All of us were like sheep that were lost, each of us going his own way. But the Lord made the punishment fall on him, the punishment all of us deserved" (Isaiah 53:6).

It was very costly for Jesus, but he did it because he loved us and wanted us to be put right with God.

God has shown us how much he loves us – it was while we were still sinners that Christ died for us (Romans 5:8).

4 Good news

When we give our lives to Jesus (which means we decide to follow him – he's the boss) we cross the gap between us and God. By his death and coming to life again, Jesus has mended the damage between us and God. When we cross the bridge, we are moving into a new kingdom – the kingdom of Jesus, and we

serve a new king – Jesus. We can only make this decision because the Holy Spirit is at work in our lives. He helps us understand these things, and helps us follow Jesus. (See 'The Holy Spirit' page 8.)

5 Action needed

IF: you have already crossed the bridge, you can be sure that Jesus has received you into his kingdom.

IF: you haven't yet crossed the bridge, then here is a simple way in which you can.

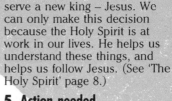

A: Admit that in God's sight you do things which are wrong, and you've got lost and separated from him.

B: Believe that King Jesus died to pay the price for what you've done wrong, and that by his coming to life again he has made it possible for you to cross the bridge into his kingdom.

C: Count the cost of crossing the bridge. It isn't easy following King Jesus – putting him first in your life, facing the laughter of your friends, putting yourself last as he did.

If you can take these three steps, then all you have to do is to decide that you want to follow Jesus and, by a simple prayer, to enter his kingdom. Here is a prayer which you can use.

Lord, I'm sorry for the past. Please forgive me. I come to you now. Please receive me into your kingdom and never let me go. Give me your Holy Spirit and, day by day, make me more like you.

Now read on, to see what Jesus wants you to do now – and tell a friend what you have done, if you have a Christian friend you can trust.

Being

One of the most common questions people ask me is, 'How can I be sure that I am a Christian?' They feel guilty about asking it, but there's no need to feel bad. God knows that we need reassuring, so here are some things which he can use to encourage you.

1 There are other Christians around

Here are the stories of two other Christians – people just like you. There are millions more like them, so read their stories, and be encouraged – Christians are ordinary people, not super-saints!

'There was a meeting at our school. Someone was coming to speak about Jesus and I wanted to go. The speaker talked very plainly about Jesus Christ, and it seemed as if every word was aimed at me – it was as if he knew me personally. But I knew that he didn't. At the end he invited anyone who wanted to give their lives to Jesus Christ to go and see him afterwards. I went, and haven't regretted it since.'

'I was on holiday and I went to a meeting where someone was speaking about Jesus. It was very interesting – in fact it sounded quite exciting – but when, at the end, he invited anyone who wanted to give their lives to Jesus to stay, I left. Part of me wanted to go back and hear more, but as I thought it over a voice inside me seemed to say, "Don't bother about going back, you don't need Christ. Think what your friends will say. Anyway it's too late now. The meeting has been over for 30 minutes. Go on home." But in the end I went back – I had to – and I gave my life to Jesus.'

2 Facts can be trusted

When I sit in a 'plane as it thunders down the runway for take off I wonder how on earth it will ever get into the air. But it does, because of the facts of aerodynamics. I might feel nervous, but the facts prove reliable every time. It's the facts of the Christian faith which make our faith secure. We may sometimes wonder, but the facts guarantee our faith. Have a look at the page called 'What do I believe about Jesus?' (page 18) for many of the facts of our faith. Here they are briefly:

- Jesus was Mary's son (Matthew 1:25).
- He was God in human form (John 1:14).
- He lived a perfect life (2 Corinthians 5:21).
- He showed the way to a new sort of life – peace, power, security, eternal life, forgiveness. We needed it, because we were lost, we'd gone against what God says and we had cut ourselves off from God (Romans 3:23).
- Jesus died (Mark 15).
- He came alive again (Mark 16).
- He is alive today (Matthew 28:20).
- His death had a purpose – to put us right with God: to forgive all that we'd done wrong and to give us a new start. His coming alive again proved that he had really done it.

SURE

LINK: Knowing Jesus for yourself (page 4)
Tough going (page 28)

3 Jesus is changing you

When we come to Jesus, he changes us. Only he can do it. Take a look at the changes that are appearing in your life. They will encourage you to believe that he is really with you. Here are some of the areas to look at – and you might find others as well.

• We *stop* living to please ourselves entirely, and we start considering others.
• We *start* wanting to know Jesus' will for our lives.
• We *start* wanting to share our new found faith with others – even if we find it difficult.
• We *stop* doing the wrong, damaging and hurtful things that we have been doing.
• We *start* learning from older Christians.

One of the key ways in which we see changes is that we begin to see answers to our prayers. What things are you praying for? Make a list of your prayers – and when you get answers, write them down. This will encourage you to believe that Jesus really has accepted you and is working in you. (Sometimes it seems that God doesn't answer our prayers, and we get hurt and confused. See page 14 about this.)

4 Remember the cross

Read Matthew 14:22–32. In this story Peter got himself in real trouble, because he took his eyes off Jesus and started to look at all the problems around him – the wind and the waves. It was only when he looked back to Jesus, and called for help, that things began to get put right.

When we wonder whether we really are Christians, we need to think again about Jesus, and remember what he has done for us.

Read Mark 14 and 15. It would be really good if you and a friend read this together. Then spend a little time thinking about what Jesus has done for you. The Holy Spirit will use this time to make your faith grow strong. Do this regularly, whenever you're tempted to think that you are not a Christian.

ACTION
Find another Christian and share your stories of how you both came to know Jesus.

PRAYER
Here is a prayer which you might use.
'Lord, help me to see you more clearly in my life, help me to love you more dearly each day and help me to follow you more closely.'

The Holy Spirit

LINK: What do I believe about Jesus? (page 18)
The Trinity (page 10)
Spiritual gifts (page 80)

I went to see a friend of mine recently and found him looking under the bonnet of his car. 'I can never figure things out,' he sighed. 'All I know is that you put petrol in one end, sit in the middle, turn the key and steer the front bit! I don't usually need to know much more than that!' In many ways the Holy Spirit is best understood in the way my friend understands his car. We don't really understand how he works, but we do know that when he is doing things in us, our lives change, and we go places with God. So here I've just concentrated on some of the things we do know about him, to help you understand something about the Holy Spirit.

Who is the Holy Spirit?

Our God is really three different and distinct persons – the Father, the Son and the Holy Spirit. They are three persons, and at the same time are one God. Read these words:

Jesus said, "Go, then, to all peoples everywhere and make them my disciples: baptize them in the name of the Father, the Son, and the Holy Spirit" (Matthew 28:19).

The Holy Spirit is equal with the Father and the Son, and he is equally important to us as Christians. Don't let anyone tell you that he doesn't matter to you, or to ignore teaching about him. It's through the work of the Holy Spirit that we become Christians in the first place. And because he is the *Holy* Spirit it is through his work that we can become holy too – we become more like Jesus. Pretty important stuff!

● Pause and thank the Holy Spirit for all he has done.

How do I meet him?

If you had an invitation to meet the Queen, I know you would make sure that you arrived on time – best behaviour, best clothes! But you don't need an invitation to meet the Holy Spirit – you've met him already. When you put your trust in Jesus Christ, the Holy Spirit came to you. You can't sense him – any more than you can see the wind. But you can see the results of his being there – just like the wind.

● Pause and tell the Holy Spirit that he is truly welcome in your life. Ask him now to teach you more about himself.

What does the Holy Spirit do?

The Holy Spirit does the most exciting things. Here are some of them – look up the passages in the Bible for more detail.

The Holy Spirit helps us follow Jesus

Jesus said, "When the Holy Spirit comes upon you, you will be filled with power" (Acts 1:8). Jesus promised his followers his power, so that we can hear and do what he says, and he makes that power available to us through the Holy Spirit. We can:
● know how to speak up for Jesus when the going gets tough (Mark 13:11).
● endure hardship and pain (Acts 20:23).
● hear God through the Bible, speak to him in prayer and understand his will for our lives (John 16:12–13 and Romans 8:26–27).
● be changed, becoming more like Jesus, loving the unlovely, and forgiving our enemies (2 Corinthians 3:18).

The Holy Spirit can even give Christians the power to work miracles, like Jesus did. The Holy Spirit may give power to:
● deal with natural occurrences – like storms (Mark 4:35–41).
● feed the hungry (Mark 6:30–42).
● heal the sick and raise the dead (Mark 5:21–43).

In short, there is nothing God cannot do, and no limit to what he may choose to do through us by the power of the Holy Spirit. God wants everything about us – who we are and what we do – to show how great he is. So let's expect God to do great things in us through the Holy Spirit. Jesus even promised that not only will we be able to do the things he did, but even greater things (John 14:12), and all this through the power of the Holy Spirit! Exciting, isn't it!

The Holy Spirit gives gifts for service

The Holy Spirit gives each one of us gifts (the ability to do particular things – not a box of chocs!) to use as we work with Jesus. (You'll find some listed on the page headed 'Spiritual gifts' (page 80). Have a look also at 1 Corinthians 12.) But how do we know which gifts we have?
● Believe that God will give us a gift. The Bible makes it clear that each one of us has some gift – no one has been left out!
● Discover our gifts. This is not so hard as it seems – remember the Holy Spirit will help us understand what he has given us if we ask him, and spend time listening to him. Many Christians have been helped through worshipping God and listening to the talks that are given in church to discover the gifts God has given them. Friends can also help, by prayer and by sharing with us what they feel our gifts are.
● Don't hurry! Don't expect to get it all clear in five minutes! It takes time, often years, to discover what God has given us. It can take many more years of prayer and practice to understand how the gifts work, and what God wants us to do with them. God can't be hurried, and we have to be patient – and I speak as one who is very impatient!

My experience

On a personal note, let me say it's hard trying to describe the Holy Spirit (the best we can do is to describe him in pictures – like the wind or a purifying fire). It's like trying to describe your love for someone – difficult because love is an experience, not just a collection of facts. Being filled with the Holy Spirit is a tremendous personal experience for Christians. If you really want to serve Christ and see the church growing in depth and power then you must get to know him more each day. He's changed my life and helped me to grow more like Jesus. I love him and I thank him for it – can you do the same?

> **PRAYER**
> We need to keep on being filled with the Holy Spirit. Use this prayer.
> 'Holy Spirit, I want to serve Jesus today. Please come and fill me. Give me power to follow Jesus and to think, say and do what's right. Thank you.'

To discover the gifts of the Holy Spirit:
● believe God wants to give us one.
● ask him.

Key verse – Luke 11:13.

The Trinity

LINK: The Holy Spirit (page 8)
What do I believe about
Jesus? (page 18)

Many Christians are not clear on what they believe about
the Trinity. God has made things clear, but it's still hard to
understand. Not all Christian teachings are easy!

Read this:

After all the people were
baptized, Jesus also was
baptized. While he was praying,
heaven was opened, and the
Holy Spirit came down on him in
bodily form like a dove. And a
voice came from Heaven, "You
are my own dear Son. I am
pleased with you" (Luke
3:21–22).

The Bible teaches us that our
God is three distinct persons –
Father, Son and Holy Spirit – but
each is so bound up with the
other that they are one being. In
this story we see the one God in
three distinct persons. The Son,
Jesus, is being baptised. The
Holy Spirit is involved, and is
pictured as a dove, resting on
Jesus. The Father is involved,
speaking powerfully from heaven.
Whenever we meet God, or
speak of him, the same process
is *always* going on. If we speak
of Jesus, the Father and the Spirit
are involved. If we speak of the
Spirit, the Father and the Son are
involved. If we speak of the
Father, the Son and the Spirit are
involved. And yet the three
persons are distinct!

● Pause now and read the story
of the baptism of Jesus again.
Now thank Jesus for his presence
in your life and, as you do,
remember that when you pray to
Jesus, the Father and the Spirit
are involved. Keep this picture in
your mind and you'll always have
a way of beginning to understand
the Trinity.

What does each do?

The Father, the Son and the Spirit
all do everything! But at the same
time, each has a special function
in the Trinity.

The Father
God the Father is the creator of
the world (see Isaiah 40:21–28).
He's not a cloud, a vague spirit,
a ghost or an astronaut. He is a
personal being, who has feelings
and emotions, who can hear us,
and speak to us in a very real
way. He is very powerful, but at
the same time very loving,
especially towards those who
love and serve him. Jesus is his
only Son, and they are closer
than we can ever imagine –
Jesus speaks of his Father as
'Dad' and says many times, 'My
Father and I. . .'

● Pause right now. Look at the
creation that God has made, and
thank him for it. The verses from
Isaiah will be a great help. Thank
God also that we can speak to
him, love him and serve him.

The Son
Jesus is the Father's only Son.
This doesn't, of course, mean
that Jesus is God's Son in a
physical sense. Nor does it mean
that Jesus was created by God.
Part of what it *does* mean is that
Jesus shares in God's divine
nature. Jesus came to this earth
to show us what God the Father
is like, and to end our separation
from him (see 'Knowing Jesus for
yourself', page 18). Look at
Philippians 2:5–11. There is no
other way back to our loving
heavenly Father, except by
following the Son. The Father has
given all authority to the Son
(see Matthew 28:18). The Son is
perfectly obedient to the Father.

● Pause now. Read this verse:

This is what love is: it is not that
we have loved God, but that he
loved us and sent his Son to be
the means by which our sins are
forgiven (1 John 4:10).

Spend some time thanking Jesus for who he is, and for what he has done for you.

The Holy Spirit

The Holy Spirit, the third 'person' of the Trinity, is God's gift to us when we start to follow Jesus Christ. He's not an impersonal force, like electricity, but a personal being. He brings us power to live our lives as Jesus desires, he brings us gifts (abilities to do particular things) to use in God's service. And he helps us understand more about Jesus day by day. Although he is in us, we need to call on his power daily, by asking to be filled with the Spirit. (See 'The Holy Spirit', page 8.)

● Read this verse:

"The Helper, the Holy Spirit, whom the Father will send in my name, will teach you everything and make you remember all that I have told you" (John 14:26).

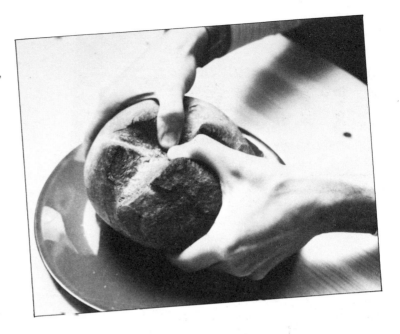

Ask the Holy Spirit right now to teach you more about himself, about Jesus, and about God the Father.

Problems?

I've never had a lot of trouble with this teaching – that's probably because I'm a simple guy! I know God as my Father, Jesus as my Lord and Saviour, and the Holy Spirit as my Helper – and the Bible teaches me that they are linked together as one being in a very special way. Before you make these pages into a paper dart, however, remember that this teaching about the Trinity has kept the Christian faith strong for thousands of years – because it describes something of what God is *really* like. So it's worth trying to understand.

LOOK INTO THE BIBLE

Two passages tell us more about the relationship between the Father, Son and Holy Spirit. They are not easy to understand on their own, but read them with the picture of the baptism of Jesus in your mind.

Jesus said, "Whoever loves me will obey my teaching. My Father will love him, and my Father and I will come to him and live with him. Whoever does not love me does not obey my teaching. And the teaching you have heard is not mine, but comes from the Father, who sent me.

I have told you this while I am still with you. The Helper, the Holy Spirit, whom the Father will send in my name, will teach you everything and make you remember all that I have told you" (John 14:23–26).

The next passage is from a letter written by the Apostle Paul to the church in Ephesus.

All things are done according to God's plan and decision; and God chose us to be his own people in union with Christ because of his own purpose, based on what he had decided from the very beginning. Let us, then, who were the first to hope in Christ, praise God's glory!

And you also became God's people when you heard the true message, the Good News that brought you salvation. You believed in Christ, and God put his stamp of ownership on you by giving you the Holy Spirit he had promised. The Spirit is the guarantee that we shall receive what God has promised his people, and this assures us that God will give complete freedom to those who are his. Let us praise his glory! (Ephesians 1:11–14).

The

◀ *The British Library hasn't got 66 books: it's got 18 million!*

I've lived in the same house for five years now, and I reckon I can find my way around with my eyes shut! But the other night we had a power cut, and I must have walked into at least six things before I got to the fuse box, and one of those things was the kitchen door! Now we've got a light fitted which only comes on when the power fails! I've fitted the light because without it I can't see to get around.

The Bible has the same purpose – to give light – for Christians. Without it we're going to walk into all sorts of things, but with it we can find our way around. One of the Psalms speaks to God about the Bible like this:

Your word is a lamp to guide me and a light for my path (Psalm 119:105).

As we use the Bible, we expect God to teach and direct us in the way we behave, and to help us know what he wants us to do for him. We don't treat it like a text book – it's a guide and a help. But it's a rather large 'lamp' – so where do we start, and how do we learn from it?

Look at the library shelves!

The Bible isn't one book, but a library of 66 books. The library is divided up, and understanding the divisions will help you get hold of the book. Here is a basic division:

The Old Testament
The 'big five' (these have quite a lot about Jewish Law): Genesis, Exodus, Leviticus, Numbers, Deuteronomy. **Histories**: Joshua and Judges through to Nehemiah. **'Writings'** (these are songs or books which give wise advice): Esther, Job, Psalms, Proverbs, Ecclesiastes, Song of Songs. The 'big four' **prophets**: Isaiah, Jeremiah (his book has a short book following it called Lamentations), Ezekiel, Daniel. The other prophets: Hosea and Joel through to Malachi.

The New Testament
The four **gospels**: Matthew, Mark, Luke, John. The **Acts of the Apostles**. St Paul's **letters** – to churches (Romans through to Thessalonians) and people (Timothy, Titus and Philemon). Letters by people other than St Paul: Hebrews through to Jude. Revelation, at the end of the Bible, is not like the other letters. It's more like a letter direct from God to us.

Three handy hints

1 Each book is divided into chapters and verses. If you see this written down: Exodus 2:3, it means 'the book of Exodus, chapter 2, verse 3'. It can get a bit confusing when there are two books of the same name. So 1 John 1:3 means the first letter of John (not the gospel of John), chapter 1, verse 3. Don't worry – even people who know the Bible quite well get this mixed up sometimes.
2 There are different versions of the Bible around today. This doesn't mean that they are different Bibles, but they are the same Bible in slightly different translations (it was originally written in Greek and Hebrew). The two you are most likely to use are the Good News Bible and the New International Version.

- The Good News Bible (often referred to by its initials – GNB). This is in an easy-to-read style and is very popular with people of every age and background. If you've not read the Bible before, this is definitely the one to go for.
- The New International Version (often referred to as the NIV). This is a good Bible for serious study. It isn't quite as easy to read as the GNB, but it follows closely the original languages in which the Bible was written.

BIBLE

3 Everyone can benefit from Bible reading notes which help us to understand the Bible better. Most notes cover three months. Why not go to your nearest Christian bookshop and check it out?

Learning from the Bible

To understand the Bible is a lifetime's job, so don't expect to get it all together in a few months – or even years. Most of us find that our knowledge grows through daily reading, and here's one way of handling a daily reading time. Find a time when you can have 15 minutes without being disturbed and:

PRAY: 'Lord Jesus, please teach me about yourself and your ways as I read this passage from your word.'

READ: the passage – if you were using the 'Use Luke' readings you might be on Luke chapter 1, verses 26–38. Read them now.

ASK: yourself – 'What have I just read?' Try to sum these thirteen verses up in a few words.

UNDERSTAND: In the story, Mary is visited by the angel Gabriel. He gives her a message from God. What is it? (See verses 31–33.) Mary is frightened at first. Why? (How would you feel if an angel visited you with a message from God!?) God gives Mary three promises to help her over her worries.

1 "Peace be with you."
2 "The angel said to her. . . . ."
3 "The Holy Spirit will come on you and. . . ."

Do things worry you? Is there anything particularly worrying you today? Well it's good news that God doesn't change. He wants us to be at peace, unafraid and full of the Holy Spirit – just what the angel said to Mary. Why not learn one of these three promises or write it on a card and keep it with you today?

THINK: Is there anything I should do, learn or pray?

PRAY: 'Thank you, Lord, for what you have taught me today. Please help me not to forget it. Amen.'

Learning alone?

Some people can manage to read and learn from the Bible on their own, but many people can't! We get stuck, bored, lost, fed up. So why not find a friend and meet, say, once a week to read the Bible together? That way you will encourage each other, and if one of you isn't very good at reading the other can help.

USE LUKE
Here's a thirty day reading plan to get you started.

Day 1, Luke 1:1–38, Preparations.
Day 2, Luke 1:39–80, Mounting excitement.
Day 3, Luke 2:1–52, Jesus' early years.
Day 4, Luke 3:1–22, Get ready.
Day 5, Luke 4:1–30, Temptation and rejection.
Day 6, Luke 4:31–44, Healing and preaching.
Day 7, Luke 5:1–31, The first followers of Jesus.
Day 8, Luke 5:32–6:19, Difficult questions.
Day 9, Luke 6:20–49, 'Love your enemies.'
Day 10, Luke 7:1–35, 'Who is this man?'

Day 11, Luke 7:36–8:21, Real love, forgiveness and obedience.
Day 12, Luke 8:22–56, The power of Jesus.
Day 13, Luke 9:1–36, 'You are God's Messiah.'
Day 14, Luke 9:37–50, True greatness.
Day 15, Luke 9:51–10:24, Working for God's kingdom.
Day 16, Luke 10:25–11:13, 'Love your neighbour.'
Day 17, Luke 11:14–53, Living as God's people.
Day 18, Luke 12:1–59, Be prepared.
Day 19, Luke 13:1–35, The narrow door.
Day 20, Luke 14:1–35, The cost of being a disciple.

Day 21, Luke 15:1–32, Lost and found.
Day 22, Luke 16:1–31, 'You cannot serve God and money.'
Day 23, Luke 17:1–37, Forgiveness, faith and the coming king.
Day 24, Luke 18:1–43, Like a child.
Day 25, Luke 19:1–48, The king is here.
Day 26, Luke 20:1–47, Jesus in danger.
Day 27, Luke 21:1–38, 'Be on your guard.'
Day 28, Luke 22:1–71, Jesus on trial.
Day 29, Luke 23:1–56, Jesus crucified.
Day 30, Luke 24:1–53, Jesus is alive.

PRAYER

Most people pray at some time in their lives, whether they believe in God or not. At times of great disaster, many people go to church who normally wouldn't do so, and those who survive disasters often say that they prayed for help while they were waiting for rescue.

Have you ever said a prayer? What were the circumstances – and what happened? Although most people have prayed at some time in their lives, not everyone admits it. Christians believe in prayer, but many of us have difficulty praying regularly, and some of us have questions we want answered first. Let's look at some.

What is prayer?

Prayer is spending time with God just as you would with a friend – sharing experiences, worries, joys and decisions in a natural way. Many of us have heard formal prayers in church. These prayers are very valuable but they are not the way in which most Christians pray daily to God. Daily prayer is relaxed and natural – just as if we were talking to a friend. Read these verses – they show how Jesus wants us to be in prayer; speaking directly to God:

'Father: May your holy name be honoured; may your Kingdom come. Give us day by day the food we need. Forgive us our sins, for we forgive everyone who does us wrong. And do not bring us to hard testing' (Luke 11:2–4).

● Pause now, and talk to God about the things that are on your mind.

Does God hear me?

Not only does God hear us, but he has left us this command in the Bible: "Call to me, and I will answer you" (Jeremiah 33:3). He is waiting to hear from us, wanting to hear from us, longing to hear from us. The problem is not with him, but with us – we don't pray because we don't really believe that he wants to hear and answer.

● Stop now, and pray to God. Tell him how you feel about things.

Does God answer prayer?

Read this verse:

"Aren't five sparrows sold for two pennies? Yet not one sparrow is forgotten by God. Even the hairs of your head have all been counted. So do not be afraid; you are worth much more than many sparrows!" (Luke 12:6–7).

LINK: Tough going (page 28)
Loving – a way of life
(page 30)
Serving – a way of life
(page 38)
Forgiving – a DIY guide
(page 52)

If God cares this much about us then he will not let our prayers go unanswered. We have to be prepared to accept that there are three possible answers to our prayers – 'Yes', 'No' and 'Wait'. It's so easy for us to feel that 'No' is not an answer to prayer, especially when we want a 'Yes'!

Is all prayer the same?
Prayer takes many different forms, depending on the circumstances. Some prayer is general – 'Father bless the families of my church' – and some is very specific – 'Father, please help John to be calm in his interview.' Some prayer is long term – 'Father, please continue to help me with my school work' – and some is very, very urgent – 'Father, we're going to have an accident unless. . .' Some prayer we do on our own, some in groups, and some in large groups. Learning to pray is like any skill – the more we do it, the better we get at it.

How do I pray?

Prayer should be natural, so having any rigid pattern of prayer can be risky. But here is a simple outline which has proved helpful to many people as they have tried to get their prayers going.

1 Praise – a time to thank God for who he is and what he has done.
2 Sorry – a time to remember what you have done wrong, and to ask God's forgiveness.
3 Thanks – a chance to remember all the things God has done for you, and to thank him. Think back over the events of the last 24 hours.

4 Please, God – a time to bring to God things that you know need changing. Pray for people as well as situations.
5 Don't forget me – prayers for our own needs.

This pattern fits easily into ten minutes a day, and that's a good length of time to start with.

PRAYER
It's good to pray with others. Why not get together with two other people and pray regularly. (Some people call this group a 'prayer triplet'.) Plan to meet for 30 minutes at least once each week to pray together.

LOOK INTO THE BIBLE
'Pray at all times' (1 Thessalonians 5:17).

ACTION
Why not get a notebook and make a note of a prayer pattern which you would like to follow for the next month?

Satan

LINK: Facing evil (page 50)

Anyone who watches the TV news or reads a paper can quickly work out that there are forces for evil in the world. The Bible says that they are headed by Satan, (also called the devil or the evil one). The Bible teaches us as much about Satan as we need to know. The main points are:

everything that's worth living for. The apostle Peter adds another side to this warning:

Be alert, be on the watch. Your enemy, the Devil, roams round like a roaring lion, looking for someone to devour (1 Peter 5:8).

Satan is a dangerous enemy and we should not take him lightly.

1 Satan is real
The image of a hairy man with horns and a tail is easy to make fun of, but don't be deceived by that into thinking Satan doesn't exist.

2 Satan is evil
Jesus is quite clear on this point. In his prayer for his followers, he asks his Father to keep us safe from the evil one (John 17:15). Everything Satan says and does is evil through and through, even though he may try to make it seem otherwise. (See also Luke 4:1–12.)

3 Satan is a deceiver
Satan is always trying to deceive us. St Paul warns us that Satan may be disguised as an angel of light (2 Corinthians 11:14). In other words, he tries to fool us into thinking that he is a force for good, and what he is asking us to do is for the good of others and ourselves. For example, it's easy to tell lies and think that we're helping people – when really we're hurting them. We need to be on our guard against this trick.

▲ *Celebrate the victory!*

4 Satan is out to destroy and spoil
Satan has only one motive in his evil heart – to spoil the work of God, and to hurt and destroy human beings, particularly those who follow Christ. Jesus himself put it this way:

"The thief comes only in order to steal, kill, and destroy" (John 10:10).

Doing wrong can seem fun at first, but it ends by breaking up

5 Satan is an accuser
One of the ways Satan works against us is to accuse us of our weaknesses. Have you ever felt these words inside you?
'You can't be a Christian, using language like that.'
'You can't be a Christian, you haven't prayed for ages.'
'You can't be a Christian, your life's in a mess.'
That's Satan at work, pointing an accusing finger at your weaknesses, and trying to make you feel it's hopeless.

6 Satan never rests
His is a permanent job – accusing, hurting, destroying, lying, cheating – day and night.

Help!!

How can we hope to survive as Christians? The Bible teaches us three main responses to Satan.

1 Jesus has won!!

When Jesus died on the cross he defeated Satan and broke his power. Read this verse:

On that cross, Christ freed himself from the power of the spiritual rulers and authorities; he made a public spectacle of them by leading them as captives in his victory procession (Colossians 2:15).

In the ancient world, when a general won a battle he would lead his prisoners in chains through his home town, while all the people came to cheer his victory. In the same way, by dying on the cross, Jesus defeated Satan and now leads him in a victory procession. We should be cheering the victory of our king, and never lose a moment to tell again the victory of Jesus against Satan. He is still a powerful force, but a broken one. We still need to take care, but we need not be afraid.
• Spend some moments thinking about the victory of Jesus over Satan. Thank God for Jesus!

2 Be filled with the Holy Spirit

We need the power of Jesus in our lives every day. Only the Holy Spirit can give us this power (see 'The Holy Spirit', page 8). It's vital that Christians keep on being filled with the Holy Spirit.
• Ask God to fill you with his Holy Spirit now.

3 Be armed and alert

Good soldiers are always on guard. Christians must do the same. So, how do we take guard?
• Know about the enemy. It's important to know the things I've written above, especially the Bible verses.
• Know yourself. If you have weak points – perhaps thoughts, actions or feelings – ask God to make you stronger. What situations in your life give Satan the best opportunity? (It could be – when you lose your temper, stop reading the Bible, have trouble praying, are confused about a girl/boyfriend, etc.) Ask God to help you in that particular situation.
• Wear the armour. Every soldier needs armour, and the Christian soldier is no exception. St Paul outlines the Christian armour in Ephesians 6:14–17.

So stand ready, with truth as a belt tight around your waist, with righteousness as your breastplate, and as your shoes the readiness to announce the Good News of peace. At all times carry faith as a shield; for with it you will be able to put out all the burning arrows shot by the Evil One. And accept salvation as a helmet, and the word of God as the sword which the Spirit gives you.

• Read the Bible. The truths of the Bible are your defence against Satan – make sure you know where to find them in your Bible. (See 'What do I believe about Jesus?' page 18.)
• Know about Jesus. What Jesus has done for you on the cross is where you can get strength to stand against evil. It's important to know all about this – read Mark chapters 14 and 15.
• Trust in God. Your faith in Jesus is a shield, to deflect all the attacks of the enemy. Make sure you look to Jesus when things get hard, and not at the enemy.

▲ Put on the whole armour of God …

Remember:
• Jesus has all authority (Philippians 2).
• Jesus has called you to himself.
• Nothing can separate you from him.
• Satan is defeated.
• We all sin.
• God understands.
• Nothing can separate him and us.
• Confess and repent.
• Rejoice.

What do I believe

These pages bring together many of the things we believe about Jesus. Use them to help you as you learn more about the Christian faith. Use them to help explain what you believe about Jesus to your friends.

The facts

- Jesus was born in the Middle East in a town called Bethlehem. His mother's name was Mary. Jesus was conceived in Mary's womb supernaturally – she was a virgin. Joseph became Mary's husband. Although he wasn't physically the father of Jesus he acted in every other way as a father towards Jesus. See Luke 1 and 2; Matthew 1 and 2.
- Jesus grew up in Nazareth. We know very little of this period. See Matthew 2:22–23.
- Jesus was baptised by John the Baptist. See Matthew 3:13–17; Mark 1:9–11; Luke 3:21–22. After

this Jesus began to travel through Galilee teaching the people about God.

Jesus' work can be divided into several different parts.

1 What Jesus said
Jesus taught about how to live to please God, how to treat others, what moral standards he expected, how and who to forgive. People were amazed at his teaching. See Matthew 5–7.

2 What Jesus did
Jesus was a man of power – over nature, sickness, demon possession, and death. He never used his power for his own ends,

nor to impress people or force them to believe. See Mark 1–10 (and especially chapter 5 for some of what Jesus did).

3 How Jesus lived
Jesus lived simply. He didn't have lots of possessions or store up wealth (see Luke 9:58). He trusted God to provide everything he needed. He had a great love for people, and had a deep compassion on people in trouble (see Matthew 9:35–38). He never refused his help to those who genuinely asked for it. Even his enemies could find nothing wrong with his lifestyle (see John 8:46). Jesus spoke strongly

about Jesus?

against those who pretended to believe, who distorted the law of God, or who led others astray (see Matthew 23).

4 Jesus' death
The death of Jesus occupies a large amount of the Gospels. (If you read Mark 14 and 15 you will have the basic facts.)
The sequence is:
- The Last Supper.
- Jesus prays in Gethsemane.
- He is betrayed and arrested.
- Jesus is tried by the Jewish council.
- He is tried by Pilate.
- The crucifixion.
- Jesus is buried.

5 Jesus' resurrection
Three days after his death, Jesus was alive again. He was seen by Mary, by the disciples going to Emmaus, by the eleven remaining disciples on various occasions, and by 500 people at once. By the way Jesus behaved, all these people believed that:
- this was the same Jesus who had died.
- this was a real person, not a ghost.

The disciples were convinced. In the following 2000 years, millions have agreed with them. For the facts see Matthew 28; Mark 16; Luke 24; John 20 and 21.

6 Jesus' ascension
This was a visible way of showing that Jesus had gone back to be with God the Father. It was only when Jesus was not physically on earth that he could be present with all his disciples, in every place, and could send the Holy Spirit to us. The ascension happened at Bethany. The disciples saw this as a joyful moment. See the end of Luke, and also the beginning of Acts.

Who is Jesus?
Because of these basic and reliable facts we can say what we believe about Jesus. Here are the key things:

1 Jesus is God
He was God before he became a baby, he was God in human form here on earth, and he still is God in heaven. This doesn't mean that he was just pretending to be a man here on earth. He was fully human, with the need to eat, sleep, etc, but at the same time he was fully God. See John 1 – a hard passage to understand, but very important to Christians.

2 Jesus is the only way to God
We believe that Jesus has shown us what God the Father is like. He has shown us the way to be right with God. We believe that there is no other way back to the Father but by what Jesus has done. (See 'Other faiths', page 76, and John 14:6.)

3 The importance of the cross
We believe that by dying on the cross Jesus was paying the price of our sins. He died in our place so that we might become God's children and serve him here on earth. Jesus' death was not the end – and the resurrection not only shows that Jesus has the power over death but shows that we can trust all he said and did. However, we can have peace with God only if we follow Jesus. (See 'Knowing Jesus for yourself', page 4, and Romans 5:1–11; 2 Corinthians 5:16–20; 1 Peter 1: 18–25.)

4 Jesus shows us how to live

We believe that Jesus expects us to model our lives on his life. We are to be concerned for the poor, the hurt, the sick, the lonely and those facing injustice. We are to try, with the help of the Holy Spirit, to be like him. That's why we read the Bible, listen to teaching, read books and watch videos about him. We are to be like him in every way. See John 13:1–17 and Mark 10:35–45.

5 Jesus and the Bible

Jesus treated the Bible as the word of God. If we follow him we'll want to think about the Bible in the same way. As we read the Bible and study it regularly God is able to speak to us today – guiding, directing and encouraging us. See Matthew 7:24–27 and 2 Timothy 3:16–17. If people say things about God and Jesus that are different from what the Bible says, we have every right not to believe them.

6 Jesus and prayer

We believe in praying often to God. We believe that by doing this we are following his example. We also believe that God hears us, wants to hear us, and answers our prayers as he sees best. We believe that prayer changes things.

7 Jesus and the plan of our lives

We believe that Jesus has a plan for our lives and for the world. We want to live by that plan. However, we have free choice, so it's possible for us to disobey or ignore the plan. If we do, we wander away from his path and his care, but he always wants to come and rescue us (Luke 15).

What do I believe *about Jesus?*

LOOK INTO THE BIBLE
Every picture needs a frame. All the facts in these pages need a frame, and the best frame is the Bible. Read **all** of Mark's Gospel in a week. Let the stories sink into your mind. It's good to do this with a friend — or how about a 'read-in' at church or in your Christian group?

8 Jesus and suffering

It's a joy to follow Jesus and to be loved by him. But it doesn't mean we'll have an easy time. Christians have to face hard times, suffering and finally death, just like everyone else. Christ can heal physical and emotional hurt, and he does – but not always. He doesn't cushion us from tough times. Remember his own words: "If anyone wants to come with me, he must forget self, carry his cross, and follow me" (Mark 8:34). But we believe that *through* times of suffering we will know the strength of Jesus (see Hebrews 13:5–6) and that there will be an end to it (Romans 8:18–19). We also have the courage to believe that he can and does use *all* things for good for those who love him (Romans 8:28). This is easy to write, but much harder to hold on to when everything seems to be going wrong. See John 15:18–25.

9 Jesus and death

We believe that Jesus has destroyed the power of death. (See Hebrews 2:14 and 1 Corinthians 15:50–58.) We will all die, but those who trust Jesus have nothing to fear because we will pass into his presence forever. We will not face the judgment (John 5:24) because all our sins have been forgiven by the death of Jesus (see 'Knowing Jesus for yourself', page 4). The Bible tells us that we will go to heaven, but leaves the details vague. It's enough for us to know that we are going there and will be with God forever.

10 Jesus and the end of the world

We believe that just as Jesus ascended into heaven, so he will come back again in the same way, to bring history to an end and to call to himself all who belong to him. (See 1 Thessalonians 4:13–18.) We don't know when this will happen, but we live in the expectation of it happening at any time. So we need to be ready. (See 1 Thessalonians 5:1–11.) Those who love Jesus have nothing to fear. We need not worry about missing his coming. It will be a major happening and there will be no mistaking it. (See Mark 13:24–27.) So ignore those people who claim to be Christ: he's not coming back again as a baby.

11 Jesus and miracles

We believe that Jesus has power over all things – including sickness, evil, nature and death. During his life he showed his power over these things. We believe that even today Jesus can and does heal people of their diseases. He doesn't appear to heal everyone, or heal instantly always. But that he can and does heal today is clear from evidence of people all over the world. (See Mark 5 and 'Miracles', page 74.)

How Should I Live –

AT SCHOOL

LINK: Loving – a way of life (page 30)
Forgiving (page 52)
Sharing Jesus – living and loving (page 82)

It's very tempting to be a part time Christian. Part time Christians are spared a lot of the problems of full time Christians. This is how they operate:

The Christian part

I'm a Christian on Sundays, when I'm with other Christians, or when I'm in a Christian group or Bible study. I pray on my own, and read my Bible when no one can see me. I know I must let Jesus control my behaviour, language and thoughts. It's hard, but I know it's what he wants.

The other part

When I'm at school, or with my non-Christian friends I keep very quiet about being a Christian. The things I learn on Sundays, and in my Christian groups I conveniently forget. I laugh at bad jokes, swear, hurt people, don't care about those in need, concentrate on myself, and on being 'in' with others. It's much easier this way – I don't have to stand against the crowd, care about unlikeable or unpopular people, or make hard decisions.
● Have you ever been tempted to be a part time Christian?

There's one big problem with being a part time Christian – it isn't what God wants! He wants you to be his follower all the time – wherever you are, and whatever you are doing. Jesus said this:

"Love the Lord your God with all your heart, with all your soul, with all your mind, and with all your strength" (Mark 12:30).

And we're to do this all the time, wherever we are. It's so easy to think that this doesn't apply to school. But if school is the place where God has put you, then that's the place to start living for him so that others can see your faith and be challenged by it. It's going to be hard for you at school just as it's hard for me in my place – and for every Christian, wherever they are. How can the Bible encourage us? Let's have a look.

Think positive

The Old Testament story of Esther makes very good reading for Christians in the 20th century. Just like many of us, she was in a very tight spot. She was Jewish and was married to the king of Persia. The king was not aware that Esther was Jewish. One day the king signed a law saying that all Jews were to be put to death. Esther was asked by the other Jews to persuade the king to change his mind.

Pretty straightforward, you think? But there was one big snag – anyone who went into the king's presence without being sent for faced immediate execution. What could Esther do? (Have you ever found yourself in a position where whatever you

decided to do you would be in for trouble from your friends?) Esther didn't give up under pressure. She took a very positive view: "I will go to the king, even though it is against the law. If I must die for doing it, I will die" (Esther 4:16). Esther saw her situation as an opportunity to serve God. She was ready to take the risks involved – in spite of the consequences.

Like Esther, God has put you where you are so that you can serve him. As far as he is concerned, you are in the right place, however tough it is. So:
● start taking a positive view. When it gets really tough, pray, 'Lord you have put me here for a purpose. Show me what it is, and help me to serve you.'
● let school be a place where you really grow as a Christian. It's your full time occupation – let it be God's school of growth for you. God *can* use things we don't like to teach us more about him.
● use school as a place to make friends for Jesus. Perhaps they will see him in you, if you are willing to become their friend.

Living prayer

God has taught us to pray at *all* times, yet often we just pray at set times. Learn to pray at different times of the day for the people around you, about the events you are passing through, and about the things that are hurting you. This kind of prayer makes life seem so much more useful, and will change your attitude to prayer.

It's tough!

A friend of mine said recently, 'When I was about 11 my friends knew that I was a Christian, and they used to laugh, and make fun, and push me around. At first I was sad but it worked out that the opposition made me more firm in my faith.' It is tough being a Christian at school, but at least you know that you are on God's front line, as much as Christians in parts of the world where Christians are persecuted.

How Should I Live –

LINK: Loving – a way of life (page 30)
Serving – a way of life (page 38)
Forgiving (page 52)

AT HOME

Some Christians have to live in really tough conditions – they are being beaten, imprisoned and even killed for their faith in Jesus. It will never be as hard for us – or will it? There's one place where it can be very tough being a Christian, and that is in your home, and with your family.

Of course you're not going to get shot at home for believing in Jesus, but it can still be hard because:
- at home everyone knows what you're really like – no pretending will fool anyone.
- at home everyone knows how you behave. When it's your turn to wash up, when you're late in, when you're under pressure – everyone will see the real you.
- at home you are closer to people than anywhere else in your life – you share the same kitchen, same table, same bathroom. In this closeness tempers can so easily flare and unforgiveness grow.
- at home people find it hardest to accept that you're changing because you love Jesus. Spiteful remarks like, 'Call yourself a Christian!' can really hurt.
- at home the pressures that come with growing up can be greatest, especially if you can't get the freedom you want and you don't like being disciplined.

What are the guidelines for a Christian living at home? Before you look at these, make a list of the good things about your home and the areas that cause you difficulty.

First rule: love . . . love . . . love

"As I have loved you, so you must love one another" (John 13:34).

This is a big challenge, because he loved us so much that he gave his life for us. This is how he expects us to love those we live closest with – brothers, sisters, parents, relatives. It's not going to be easy is it?

What's more, sometimes we have to go on loving people even though we don't *feel* love towards them. There are occasions when we have to remember that Christ commands us to love despite how we feel.

This looks hard, and it is hard, but many have found that this kind of love can be very rewarding.
- Do you love those you live with? Ask Jesus right now to show you how to love them. Pray every day for them, and take every opportunity to show God's love to them.

Second rule: forgiveness rules OK

In the closeness of home life, it's vital that we have a forgiving heart. Jesus taught us to pray: 'Forgive us our sins, as we forgive everyone who does us wrong.' This has got to be our attitude.
- Do you forgive and forget, or bear a grudge? Are there things that you have got to go and ask forgiveness for right now? Ask God to give you courage and strength.

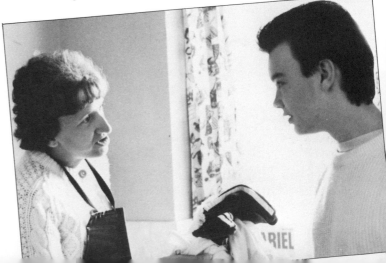

RVING

...can become a servant of my ...amily by:
1. taking my turn at family chores without complaining.
2. offering to do things without being asked.
3. offering to do chores for others occasionally.
4. looking out for opportunities to help others.
5. keeping my eyes fixed on Jesus, who became a servant, and trying to follow his example. (See John 13:1–17.)

Third rule: do it God's way

Not only do we have to be honest and open in our relationships in our homes, we've got to live by the truths of the Bible. This means, for example:

- we honour our parents.
- we are willing to be servants of others in our homes. A servant is not a doormat but a person who willingly puts the needs of others before him/herself.
- we pray for others at home.
- we willingly forgive.
- we love those with us in our homes.
- we share what we have with those in our homes.

There are many other biblical truths that we need to live out. If we can't live them at home, how can we pretend to live them in the world?

- Do you honour your parents? What do you think this will involve?
- Are you willing to be a servant, or do you always insist on your rights?

Fourth rule: encourage one another

Barnabas (see Acts 4:36) means 'one who encourages'. He was given a difficult job – to go to Antioch and check up on what was happening. But when he saw what God was doing, he *encouraged* the Christians there. We need to be encouragers in our homes. There's so much discouragement around.

Everyone gets discouraged sometimes – make it your job to be a Barnabas, one who encourages the rest of the family. This isn't something you can 'put on'. It has to come from your Christian convictions, and it has to be genuine. But you'll soon find the joy in encouraging others. And you'll find that you're being encouraged yourself.

God has placed us in families – we're not in them by accident. God wants your family to grow in faith and love, and he's put you there to be able to use you to make this happen. You may live in a divided family, or even have seen your family break up. God can still use you to encourage and bless your family.

FAMILY BUILDING

1 Pray every day for each member of your family by name.
2 Pray for the whole family: 'Holy Spirit, come into my home today. Use me as a channel of your blessing to the people I live with.'
3 Look out for opportunities to encourage each family member once – 'Mum, you look nice', 'Thanks for the lift to school, Dad', 'Thanks for lending me your shirt, Dave'. . .

Living – *when I feel*

However careful we are, we all occasionally get things wrong. Whether it's homework, cake making, or map reading – it's always possible to make mistakes.

This is as true for our spiritual life as it is for our daily life. God has a plan for us, but occasionally we step outside it. How does God feel about this, and what can we do about it? The story of the fall and rise of Peter, a close disciple of Jesus, will give us some clues.

The fall

Peter was one of the closest followers of Jesus. He had been called by Jesus (see Mark 1:16–20, but don't be confused by the fact that this passage uses Peter's 'old' name, Simon). He had seen all the great miracles, heard all the great teachings and, what's more, was living daily with Jesus. Surely he couldn't get things wrong! Unfortunately:

● he ignored Jesus' warning (read Mark 14:27–31). Jesus tried to tell Peter that he was in danger of denying his faith, but he was too sure of himself to listen.
● he failed (read Mark 14:66–71). When Jesus was arrested Peter followed him into the courtyard of the High Priest. But when he was challenged, "You, too, were with Jesus of Nazareth," he denied it. It was dark, he had just seen his master arrested, and he was afraid. That's quite natural, but if he had listened to Jesus' warning earlier . . .? Twice more he denied Jesus and then, realising what he had done, he broke down and cried.

Restored!

When Jesus came alive again from the dead he met with his disciples on a number of occasions. On one of these, he asked Peter three times, "Do you love me?" (see John 21:15–17). When Peter says that he does, Jesus gives him a challenging and vital job: "Feed my sheep." In other words, Jesus gives Peter a key job in the church. Would you have put a man like Peter in charge, after what he had done? Jesus did just that – and Peter did become one of the leading early Christians. The lesson from the fall and rise of Peter is simple – we can all fail, but God doesn't reject us, he restores us and goes on using us as he did before. Sometimes he even opens up new things for us to do. Exciting, isn't it?

I've lost my way

LINK: Being sure (page 6)

Finding your way back

- Have you ever felt that you've slipped away from God's plan?
- Do you feel that way right now?
- Do you have a friend who feels this way?

Then learn a lesson from Peter – it will be a great encouragement to anyone who has lost their way. This is how it works:

1 Know you are lost

I travel about a lot by car and I'm often in strange towns, where I easily get lost. I get very angry with myself and drive round and round. Eventually I stop and admit that I am lost. This is the first step to finding the right way – I can never get it right while I'm whizzing around. Peter had a clear warning from Jesus, but didn't listen. He didn't know that he was losing his way. He only found out that he was lost after this third denial – and then he broke down and cried.

- Are you lost? The best thing in the world you can do is to stop and admit it to God. It's the beginning of the way back, as Peter discovered.

2 Know whose fault it is

Peter knew. He began to cry because he knew that it was his fault – his alone. Are you willing to admit that it's your fault? There's a 'sorry' prayer on this page – why not use it now? Perhaps you're too proud to admit that you're lost – then you'll never find your way back. Is your pride worth that much to you?

LOOK INTO THE BIBLE
Read Isaiah 12 and Psalms 8 and 46.

---

3 Be restored

God doesn't bear a grudge. He isn't going to say: 'So at last you admit it's your fault. Well, serves you right! You can just stay lost a bit longer, and then I might find a job for you. But mark my words, I won't forget this mistake!' Quite the opposite, as Peter found out. You're welcomed back with open arms and put back on the right path. God doesn't bear grudges – he's glad to have you back. There's a 'thank you' prayer on this page – why not use it now?

4 Listen

Peter didn't need to get lost. God warned him, but he wasn't listening. God will direct you, if you will give time to hear him. Through prayer, using the Bible, and sharing with friends, we can all keep our lives fixed on God's pathway for us.

'SORRY' PRAYER
'Lord, I'm lost. I'm sorry, and I know it's my fault. Just as you forgave Peter, please forgive me. Show me what to do now, and send me help.'

'THANK YOU' PRAYER
'Lord, I want to thank you for being so loving and caring to me. I know I don't deserve it, and yet you go on loving me and caring for me. I want you to know that I really am thankful.'

Tough

LINK: Being sure (page 6)

Do you find it easy to be a Christian? What do you find to be the hardest thing?

Choose from this list:
- Things I do wrong, and feel bad about.
- Things I say – my language.
- The way I treat others.
- Selfishness, greed, envy, anger.
- Doubt, worry, fear – is God really in charge?
- Bad sexual thoughts.
- Having to love and care for others all the time.
- Being a servant of others.
- Caring for the poor.
- Having to live for Jesus in front of people who either don't care, or who laugh at me.
- Having to forgive others.
- Going to church, praying, reading the Bible.
- Getting on with others at church.
- The constant accusation of Satan: 'You're not a real Christian/if you really were a Christian you wouldn't do that/you're not forgiving enough/you don't pray enough.'

It's a tough looking list isn't it, and the bad news is that we will be facing some of these difficulties every day, because it *is* tough being a Christian. Jesus warned us about it when he said, "If anyone wants to come with me, he must forget self, carry his cross, and follow me" (Mark 8:34).

Why is it tough?

1 Christians are different!
As Christians we are trying to live by Christian standards. We *do* want to be changed to be like Jesus; we *do* want to change society so that it is more as

Jesus wants it. This leads inevitably to resentment, even hatred, from those who like the world the way it is. See John 15:18 – although the world is really hating Jesus ('world' here means those things and people around who are against God), it will take it out on us.

2 We have an enemy
As we have already seen, Christians are faced by a deadly enemy – Satan (see page 16). He never stops opposing God's work, and that means attacking us as a way of attacking God. He attacks us by accusing us (that's where all the 'you can't be a Christian' stuff comes from) and by attacking us through doubt, uncertainty, worry, fear, and sometimes through other people.

3 It just IS!
This verse from St Paul's letter to the Ephesians says it all:

For we are not fighting against human beings but against the wicked spiritual forces in the heavenly world, the rulers, authorities, and cosmic powers

of this dark age. So put on God's armour now! Then when the evil day comes, you will be able to resist the enemy's attacks; and after fighting to the end, you will still hold your ground (Ephesians 6:12–13).

In the end, it is tough being a Christian. It has always been this way and it always will be. We have to accept it as a fact of life.

What can we do to stand it?

1 Don't lose heart
We find it tough, and we often want to give up – at least I do (look at 2 Corinthians 4). But our Christian faith does not depend on *us* keeping going. We belong to Christ because of his death on the cross. If we have said 'Yes' to him, nothing – absolutely nothing – can separate us from his love. Have you found it too tough, and given up? Then read this verse and remember that God loves you and will never let you go.

For I am certain that nothing can separate us from his [God's]

going

love: neither death nor life, neither angels nor other heavenly rulers or powers, neither the present nor the future, neither the world above nor the world below – there is nothing in all creation that will ever be able to separate us from the love of God which is ours through Christ Jesus our Lord (Romans 8:38–39).

2 Be prepared

Soldiers know that battles are going to be tough – so they keep in training. We're in a battle and, as God's soldiers, we need to be prepared to face hard times. Our training?

- Daily times of prayer – this is essential. (See 'Prayer', page 14.) Have you stopped praying? Don't feel guilty about it, but instead start again today – even right now.
- Daily use of the Bible – this isn't always easy, because the Bible is a big book and it needs time spent on it. (See 'The Bible', page 12.) Given up? Then start again right now. Start with Mark's Gospel (the second book in the New Testament) and read five verses a day for the next week. Ask God to teach you something new each day. (Sometimes it's much easier to read and learn from the Bible with a friend, or in a group.)

> **LOOK INTO THE BIBLE**
> Read Ephesians 6:1–11.

Be prepared!

- Weekly worship – we all need times with other Christians where we can worship God together. Given up going to church? Then make a new start this week. Do you have a friend who goes to church? Then why not go along with him or her. It doesn't matter to God that it isn't your regular church.

3 Keep awake

We are easily lulled into a false sense of security. We think that everything is going well, and that it won't get tough for us. But it will! The enemy is like a lion, looking for someone to kill (1 Peter 5:8). So keep on guard! Keep praying, listening to God, and letting the Holy Spirit work in you every day.

4 Jesus has won!

On the cross, at Calvary, Jesus defeated Satan and broke his power. Read this:

On that cross, Christ freed himself from the power of the spiritual rulers and authorities; he made a public spectacle of them by leading them as captives in his victory procession (Colossians 2:15).

In the ancient world, when a general won a battle he would lead his prisoners in chains through his home town, while all the people came to cheer his victory. Jesus has won the battle and so we should be cheering the victory of our king and celebrating the victory of Jesus over Satan.

HELP!
1 Don't lose heart.
2 Be prepared.
3 Keep awake.
4 Jesus has won!

Loving –
a way of life

LINK: Forgiving (page 52)

Are you a 'do-it-yourselfer'? Those books that tell you how to do it always look so easy, but as soon as I try to do it all the wires and pipes seem back to front! Dieting seems to be just the same – very easy in theory, but very painful in practice!

It's the same with wanting to be more loving towards others. We know God wants it, because the Bible tells us so. Because we want what God wants we want to be more loving. It's easy to say, but tough to do, because we are basically very selfish and want our own way most of the time. It's vital at the outset of this section to realise that we cannot make ourselves love others – only God can do it for us. Here's a prayer that you might like to use, now and daily:

> Lord Jesus, I want to love others and be a more loving person. But I can't do it myself. Please work in my life.

Ask yourself:
- Who do I love most in the world?
- Why do I love them so much?
- Who do I dislike and why?

1 Loving people can be risky

Read Luke 15:11–14.

The story
The younger of the two sons asked his father for his share of the family business. As soon as he got it he sold it and left home. He then had the time of his life – until the money ran out.

The questions
- How do you think the father felt about the request to split up the family business?
- What would you have done?

The lesson
The father let his son have his way. This was very costly – not only did the father lose a big part of his business; he also must have known what his son was like and what would happen to the money. But he also knew that the son had to learn for himself.

The lesson is that if you love people you risk getting hurt. In trying to love others we will feel and experience pain – the pain of rejection, hostility, and even ridicule. There is no way round this fact, and it has to be accepted, or we won't ever be able really to love people.
- Ask God to help you bear the hurt.
- If it gets too tough, read the story of Jesus' love in Mark 14 and 15.

2 Love never gives up

Read Luke 15:15–24.

The story
The son had a good time till he'd blown all the cash. Then all his friends deserted him and he was reduced to keeping pigs. He was so hungry that he even felt like eating the pig swill. At this point he decided to go back home, apologise to his dad, and ask for a job as a servant in his father's house. He felt that he had lost the right to be a son.

The questions
- If you were the father, what would you have felt once your son had left with the money?
- If you were the father, would you want him back?
- If you were the father, on what terms would you have accepted him back?

The lesson
The father had been looking out for his son, hoping against hope

that he would return. He knew his son had made a mistake but he carried on hoping, waiting, looking out. And when the son appeared he offered acceptance, welcome and love. He didn't give him a lecture, or threaten punishment if it should ever happen again. The son, after all, had learnt his lesson.

This is what love is all about – never giving up on people, never bearing a grudge, forgiving freely and with joy. It's tough, and it takes a lot of work by God on our lives to make us like this father. But this is God's aim for us – do you want to be like this?

3 It's hard to believe!

Read Luke 15:25–32.

The story

The son could hardly believe it! No sooner had he got his confession out than he was dressed in the best robes and was having a welcome-home feast! Sadly, not everyone agreed with the father's generous love. The eldest son refused to even come to the celebration, muttering, 'Look, all these years I have worked for you like a slave, and I have never disobeyed your orders. What have you given me? . . . . But this son of yours wasted all your property on prostitutes, and when he comes back home, you kill the prize calf for him!' (Luke 15:29–30.)

The questions
● How do you feel about the actions of the father?
● How do you think the younger son felt?
● Why did the elder son feel like he did – was he right?

The lessons
God's love has no strings attached to it. He doesn't threaten to recall all our failures when we are wrong, and he does promise a welcome whenever we have fallen away and return. The question is – can we love others in this way, in such a way that they can hardly believe it?

LOOK INTO THE BIBLE
Read 1 Corinthians 13.

CHECK IT OUT
Read this passage: Fill in the blanks with your name.
.... is patient and kind.
.... is not jealous or conceited or proud.
.... is not ill mannered or selfish or irritable.
.... does not keep a record of wrongs.
.... is not happy with evil, but is happy with the truth.
.... never gives up.
...........'s faith, hope and patience never fail.
Is this the kind of love you're willing to offer other people? Ask the Holy Spirit to show you how to grow in love.

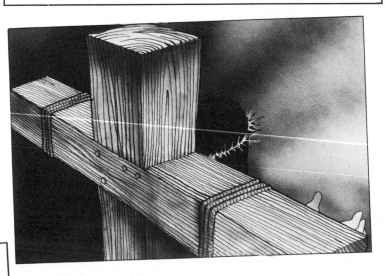

BOY *meets* GIRL

LINK: Sex (page 54)
Abortion (page 68)

Imagine you're an agony aunt or uncle. How would you answer this letter?

'I'm six feet tall, assertive and strong. I can even bend iron bars with my teeth. I love eating garlic. Why can't I get a girlfriend?'
                                                        Troubled of Newcastle.

Not many people can bend iron bars with their teeth! But most of us have a problem when it comes to getting it right with members of the opposite sex. Here are some you may have come up against. . . .

• You've tried and failed, you're afraid of getting hurt again.
• You're unsure of your sexual reactions . . . will things get out of hand? How can you keep control?
• You get embarrassed – and say and do the wrong things.
• You think everyone else has a boy/girlfriend except you. So you feel bad and lack any confidence with the opposite sex.
• Your parents keep interfering and don't seem to understand.
• You're trying to live up to the image of relationships given on TV and in the popular press, plus pressure from your friends.

If this is you – the Bible contains some good news!

God loves you

It's easy to get in a muddle about the opposite sex and to feel bad if things aren't working out. But remember; God loves you for yourself, whether you have a boy/girlfriend or not. You are valuable and precious to him for who you are, not for who you go out with.

God made us for each other

Men and women were made to be together. The Bible says, 'For this reason a man will leave his father and mother, and unite with his wife, and the two will become one' (Mark 10:7). That's God's plan – for the happiness and joy which each partner can give to the other in marriage. If God made it that way, he will help you get things right. Be patient!

God has rules, designed to help

● Be pure. (See Psalm 24:4.) With so much rubbish and so many rotten examples around it's hard for us to keep our hearts and minds clean. But if we don't, then all our thinking and behaviour can be spoilt. It's vital that we come to God regularly, to confess anything that has been impure and to ask him to make us clean. This verse from the Bible encourages us to believe that this is God's plan:

If we confess our sins to God, he will keep his promise and do what is right: he will forgive us our sins and purify us from all our wrongdoing (1 John 1:9).

● Check with him. It's not easy to know what is right and what is wrong, however careful we are. But God knows right from wrong and will always give us the help and direction we need (see James 1:5). Get into the habit of praying wherever you are or whatever you are doing. Asking, 'Father, is this right?' will bring guidance and direction.

● Be practical. If God came into the room right now, would you be ashamed of what you are thinking or doing? This question, which I first heard many years ago, has again and again helped me to think straight about sexual matters.

STANDARDS

Everyone is made in the image of God. I enjoy them for who they are, not for what I can get from them.

Relationships are to do with feelings – I need to be careful I don't hurt someone.

Lust, pornography, bad morals – these must be recognised and rejected.

Relationships with the opposite sex are fun. God meant that way.

Put yourself in their shoes

Tom is very fond of Ann but he's never told her or shown her any affection. One day he sees her talking to another boy and gets jealous. So, spurred into action, he asks her out himself. Later in the evening he tells her how he feels about her. Ann explains she likes him as a friend, but that's all. He's upset. What advice would you give Tom?
● 'You should have got to know Ann a bit more first, before you told her how you felt about her.'
● 'Did Ann ever lead you to believe that she was fond of you?'
● 'Ann has a right to feel how she does – so why are you so upset?'
● 'You shouldn't have asked Ann out because you were jealous of someone else doing so.'

Sue and Peter, both Christians, have been going out for some time and get on well. Going home from a night out at a disco they stop and, after a few kisses, Pete tries it on . . . . but Sue refuses. What would you say to Pete if he came to you moaning that he's thinking of breaking off his relationship with Sue because she's frigid? Would you:
● suggest that his motives were wrong, and that Sue was right?
● tell him to go and apologise for his behaviour?
● tell him he was right, and that other girls will be more willing?

Sean is worried because he hasn't had a girlfriend. All the other boys in his group boast regularly about their conquests, which make him feel worse. He asks you what's wrong with him. Would you:
● point out that most of the other boys are lying – they just want to impress?
● ask him if he's had problems with girls in the past?
● tell him to be patient – opportunities will come?

Becky and Steve have been going steady for years. They love each other, but don't use this to exclude others. Both their parents know and approve. It's a good relationship. But they aren't sure about the future, as Steve is going to college. What do you think they should do?
● Get married, and then sort out the future.
● Get engaged, and then sort out the future.
● Pray and see what happens.
● Let Steve go to college, and keep in touch. After all, if they really love each other, then their love will stand the test.

It's hard to know what to do, isn't it? But God has not left us to sort it out alone, the Bible gives us guidance to know what's right. And living by God's standard's is the way to work it out.

Marriage

∞ ∞ ∞ ∞ ∞ ∞ ∞ ∞ ∞

LINK: Loving – a way of life (page 30)
Sex (page 54)

Perhaps you're not exactly thinking about getting married tomorrow! Maybe not, but most of us get married at some time in our lives and it may not be so far away as you think.

Marriage is still very popular, despite what you might read in the papers, or see on TV. Did you know, for example, that there were 350,000 marriages in England and Wales in 1986 – and that's more than in previous years. So however old (or young) you are it's important to get hold of what the Bible says about marriage – not only so that you know for yourself but so that you can share it with other people. When people aren't so sure about marriage, or suggest that it's just as good to live together, without bothering about ceremonies and lifelong commitments, you need to know what's right.

gift, earned for us by Christ on the cross. But we've also discovered that we have to work hard at our faith. With the help of the Holy Spirit we learn more and grow stronger as the years pass. Marriage is just the same. It's a gift of God which husband and wife can receive with joy. But then they have to work hard at it; to make it work and grow.

● Marriage is the place for sex and having children. God designed us as sexual beings. He gave us marriage, so that we could enjoy that sexual

Facts

● Marriage is part of God's plan. At the outset of creation we read, 'That is why a man leaves his father and mother, and is united with his wife, and they become one' (Genesis 2:24). (A better translation of 'become one' is 'become one flesh'. This gives a clear idea of the total commitment between man and woman in marriage.) The Bible teaches that marriage is not an accidental product of society, nor was it invented because it seemed a 'good idea'. It's God's plan and purpose for people.

● Marriage is a total commitment. Once we get married, we've entered into an experience that is total, permanent and lifelong. When God spoke of a man and wife becoming one flesh, that's just what he meant. With so many marriages ending in divorce, it's easy to lose sight of what God intends marriage to be.

● Marriage isn't instant. We know that our salvation is a free

∞ ∞ ∞ ∞ ∞ ∞ ∞ ∞ ∞ ∞ ∞ ∞ ∞ ∞

experience with one other person and no other. That's why sexual experience outside of marriage is wrong; it spoils the 'one flesh' relationship which we should enjoy. Within this committed, long-term relationship children can be born and feel secure.

● Marriage has got its God given pattern. God doesn't just leave us to work out marriage for ourselves. He's given clear guidelines about the relationship husband and wife are to have with each other. There's advice for husbands, wives, parents and children in Ephesians 5:21–6:4. As in all Christian relationships, we're to *serve* each other.

Submit yourselves to one another because of your reverence for Christ (Ephesians 5:21).

Think about it:

These questions may seem irrelevant to you, but it's worth having them in the back of your mind so that when they get talked about you've done a bit of thinking.

● Is marriage worth it? Some people suggest that it's just as good to live with someone you love without bothering with all the ceremony. But:
– hundreds of thousands of people in Britain don't seem to agree with this. That's why they get married.
– not bothering with marriage isn't God's pattern for us, and his pattern seems very popular, despite all attempts to do it other ways.
– those who choose to live together can very easily 'un'live together, whenever they feel like it – if, for example, they have a really big bust up. Our marriage commitment helps guard against splitting up on the spur of the moment. Even though many marriages end in divorce, far more last for life.

What do you think?
● How do I know who to marry? 'Boy meets girl' seems to be the way it happens in the films but real life isn't often like this.

There are all kinds of thing to be sorted out, and they're not silly things to ask. For example:
– what am I looking for in a future husband/wife?
– how do I know that we're going to get on together over many years?
– do I really love them – with a love that's more than just sexual attraction?
– how will we meet?
– what about a time of courting?
– how will I expect him/her to treat me?

What do you think?
● Will my marriage go wrong? Some marriages do break up – and that is very painful. What do you think you can do to make sure that, if you get married, your marriage will last? (Have a look at the 'Facts' bit on these pages.)
● Does being a Christian help? We believe that God has a major part to play in our marriages. This doesn't make everything easy, but it does give us a rock on which to build. But what part does God play? How does he make us stronger? (See the contents page for where to find other units in the 'Lifestyle' section. They'll give you some clues.)

Marriage is a lot of fun, but it's also a serious business. Husbands/wives make big promises to God, and to their wife/husband. This is it:

I, ..., take you, ..., to be my wife/husband, to have and to hold from this day forward; for better, for worse, for richer, for poorer, in sickness and in health, to love and to cherish, till death us do part, according to God's holy law; and this is my solemn vow.

∞ ∞ ∞ ∞ ∞ ∞ ∞ ∞ ∞ ∞ ∞ ∞ ∞ ∞ ∞

Temptation

LINK: Satan (page 16)
The Holy Spirit (page 8)

Cream cakes and books! These are the things which tempt me and my wife most often. She longs for a cream cake, but she knows that it will spoil her figure. I long for the latest book on computers, but know it will spoil my budget – permanently! These temptations make us smile, but there are more serious temptations that give Christians a lot of cause for thought.

For example:
- At what point does enjoying the company of the opposite sex become a temptation to lust? At what point does admiring someone else's boyfriend/girlfriend become jealousy?
- When does an apparently harmless temptation – eating, sport, having a drink – become a dangerous obsession?
- Where do these temptations come from, and why don't they go away easily? Is it a sin to be tempted, and how can I resist them? Will God reject me?

These questions do need to be faced, and the Bible gives us answers.

We are all tempted

Every test that you have experienced is the kind that normally comes to people (1 Corinthians 10:13).

The Bible teaches us that *every* Christian is tempted, often with the same sorts of temptation as other people. Even Jesus wasn't excluded from temptation (see Matthew 4:1–11). But is temptation the same as sin? A Christian once said to me, 'I keep having these bad dreams, where I am doing terrible things.

Is this a sin?' When I asked him if he wanted these dreams, he gave a very clear, 'NO!' So I encouraged him to believe that this was temptation – not sin – and that if he resisted it there would be no sin involved.
- What temptations are you facing today? What temptations have you faced in the last weeks?

Temptation is Satan's business

Temptation does not come from God. Read these words: 'for God

cannot be tempted by evil, and he himself tempts no one' (James 1:13). Temptation is Satan's work. Satan tries to pull us away from God's path by suggesting all sorts of things to us. For example, have you ever struggled with any of these:
- 'You don't need to love him – he doesn't deserve it.'
- 'Isn't she beautiful – wouldn't you like to undress her.'
- 'Look at her! Who does she think she is, going out with him. Go and tell someone how she's behaving!'
- 'He/she deserves it.'
- 'Why should I wash up?'
- 'I can't be bothered to . . . read my Bible or pray.'
- 'Why should I say sorry – it wasn't my fault.'
- 'It wasn't me.'
- 'I can't be a true Christian because I keep doing/saying things. . . . .'

Satan never stops tempting us. All the time he's there, trying to pull us away from God.

What can we do?

1 Trust God to understand
God is a forgiving God. As soon as we give in to temptation we need to turn immediately to him, say sorry, and ask for his forgiveness. (See 'Forgiveness', page 40.) As soon as we do this, we are forgiven. There's one thing you can guarantee – Satan will come and tempt you with

this: 'Forgiveness cannot be as easy as that!' That's why it's vital to link forgiveness with the Bible. Make sure you can always find 1 John 1:8–9. Read it now.
● Are there things that you need to confess to God right now? Put this book down and do it.

2 Recognise our weaknesses and stand firm
It's important to know where we can be most easily tempted. What are the areas in your life that you are most easily tempted in? I'm tempted to worry about money. I worry about whether there will be enough money to pay the various bills. It's good to know where we are weak – then we can guard that area with greater care.
● Ask God to help you stand firm against temptation in your weak areas.

3 God is with us
Temptation can be a way of training and strengthening our faith. As we learn to understand what is going on, and to resist, so we grow stronger in our faith. (See James 1:2–3.) At all times God is in it with us. Read this:

Every test that you have experienced is the kind that normally comes to people. But God keeps his promise and he will not allow you to be tested beyond your power to remain firm; at the time you are put to the test, he will give you strength to endure it, and so provide you with a way out (1 Corinthians 10:13).

Ask God to show you now how to cope with the particular temptations you face.

4 We need each other
We are all tempted. It's easy to fail to help and encourage others when they are facing temptation – yet they need our encouragement and prayers, just as we need theirs. See Galatians 6:2.
● Do you have any friends who are facing temptation right now. Pray for them and try to encourage them in some way. Remember that we all belong to the same family. We can't abandon our friends to sink or swim on their own.

SPOT IT
Ask yourself
● Where am I weak?
● Where am I tempted most often?
● Is there anything I can/should do about this?
● Is someone else praying for me about this?

VICTORY!
Remember, Jesus has defeated Satan. Read this:

And on that cross Christ freed himself from the power of the spiritual rulers and authorities; he made a public spectacle of them by leading them as captives in his victory procession (Colossians 2:15).

LOOK INTO THE BIBLE
If you ever give in to temptation you'll need to know 1 John 1:8–9. Why not learn it now?

SERVING –
a way of life

LINK: The Bible (page 12)
Prayer (page 14)
The Holy Spirit (page 8)

Sometimes, when I'm feeling a bit fed up with what I do for a living, I read the jobs ads in the paper. They all look so exciting, especially the pay! Supposing you were to write a job ad for a Christian – what would you put?

Two of Jesus' followers – James and John – wanted to be sure of getting the best jobs in God's kingdom, so they asked Jesus if they could have the most important positions. When the rest of the disciples heard of James and John's attempt to get the best jobs they were angry and a squabble broke out. When Jesus saw what was going on he said:

"If one of you wants to be great, he must be the servant of the rest; and if one of you wants to be first, he must be the slave of all. For even the Son of Man (Jesus) did not come to be served; he came to serve and to give his life to redeem many people" (Mark 10:43–45).

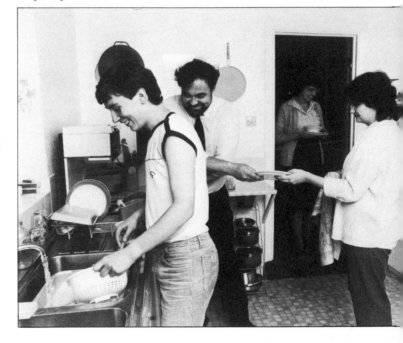

This is the job ad for a Christian – to follow Jesus by being the servant of others. Not many of us like the idea of being a servant – it sounds like it isn't going to be much fun. But the servant's job is a great honour. Why?

- Jesus came 'not to be served but to serve'. What an honour to have the same position and titles as Jesus had!
- It was the title many other famous Christians have had. Mary, when she learnt that she was to be the mother of Jesus,

said: "I am the Lord's servant; may it happen to me as you have said" (Luke 1:38).

There's no avoiding it – if we follow Jesus, then we have to follow as servants: servants of him, of each other, and of those we live and work with. It looks easy on paper, but it's not so easy to do at home, in the classroom, the office, the factory. It's even harder to serve those

who aren't particularly lovable or friendly towards us, especially when others will laugh at us, look down on us, or see us as doormats. So how can we be servants?

1 Spend time with Jesus

To be servants we have to be changed, and only Jesus can do that (see 2 Corinthians 5:17). As we pray and read the Bible,

worship and mix with other Christians, so our hearts will be changed. That's why the basic Christian disciplines of prayer, worship and listening to God's word are so important.
● Why not promise to spend more time with Jesus today?

2 Be filled with the Holy Spirit

The Holy Spirit has the job of changing us. As we learn what Jesus wants changed, we need to ask the Holy Spirit to bring those changes about.
● Here is a 'changing prayer':

Holy Spirit, I want to be changed, so that I can be a servant of others, just as Jesus was a servant. Please make those changes happen.

3 Check it out

Servants have to start serving, not just thinking about it! (See John 13:1–17.) Serving can take many different forms. Maybe you could be doing a practical job, supporting a friend, encouraging someone, helping someone in a crisis, lending something, providing a listening ear, giving some advice. It's fairly easy to see the needs that are around us.
● In the next week make a list of the opportunities you have had to help someone – including those you missed.
● Make a list during the week of occasions where you have put your needs first, and when you have failed to serve others.

At the end of each day thank God for the opportunities you've had and taken and ask his forgiveness for those you've missed.

4 Servants are tough

We can easily think that servants are weak people – doormats to be trodden on by others. If we start thinking this, we need to remember:
● only Satan wants us to think like this. (See 'Satan', page 16.) He doesn't want people to be like Jesus, and to be a servant is to be like Jesus.
● Jesus was a servant, but he was one of the toughest men that ever lived. He had the strength to die a painful death on the cross because he loved us so much. Anyone who follows his example can never be described as weak. See Philippians 2:1–11.

SERVING OTHERS

In the home –
● do the washing up (and other chores) without moaning. Why not sometimes do jobs that others should do?
● don't complain when you're hard done by. (Stop saying, 'It wasn't my fault. . . !')
● support other members of the family (especially if they're having a tough time) rather than just letting them go through it.

In daily living –
● look out for the needs of others and be willing to help meet them. (Be willing to lend and share your possessions.)
● forgive without holding a grudge (instead of making the most of it!)
● stand up for others who are being unfairly treated (especially when someone else is being spoken of unfairly, or is being hurt through no fault of their own).
● be patient with those who are awkward and aggressive (especially those in authority).
● look out for the needs of the weak and under privileged (the very young, the very old, the sick, the lonely, those who are afraid) even if it is inconvenient.
● be prepared to help those in need – by supporting a voluntary group (CARE Trust, TEAR Fund, The NSPCC, etc.).

LOOK INTO THE BIBLE
Look at Mark 10:45, Luke 1:38 and John 15:18.

Forgiveness:

LINK: Loving – a way of life
(page 30)
What do I believe about
Jesus? (page 18)
Forgiving – a DIY guide
(page 52)

When a friend of mine decided to follow Jesus she was on top of the world. But after a few months something began to worry her. She thought: 'How can I possibly be a Christian – I'm still doing and saying and thinking things that are wrong. Shouldn't this have stopped? How does God feel about me still sinning? Will he reject me now?'

● Have you ever wondered about this? Are there things which you know are not right in your life, and which worry you, making you feel that perhaps God might reject you?

Many new Christians do worry that God may reject them because they do and say things that are wrong. We need to understand the nature of God's forgiveness. This section looks at what forgiveness means from God's point of view, and what it can mean for us.

1 We're in a mess

For a start it's vital to realise that God knows exactly what we are like on the inside. Here is what the Bible says:

All of us have been sinful; even our best actions are filthy through and through (Isaiah 64:6).

"From the inside, from a person's heart, come the evil ideas which lead him to do immoral things, to rob, kill, commit adultery, be greedy, and do all sorts of evil things." (Mark 7:21–22).

Everyone has sinned and is far away from God's saving presence (Romans 3:23).

We can relax. God knows all about us. He knows that we have the potential to do much good, but he also knows that we have much inside us that is bad.

2 God loves us

God could have just left us to it, couldn't he? But he didn't. He sent us Jesus, to remove our sins and to bring us back to God. Every Christian should know these two verses by heart – they are the reason for our confidence in God's forgiveness:

"For God loved the world so much that he gave his only Son, so that everyone who believes in him may not die but have eternal life" (John 3:16).

This is what love is: it is not that we have loved God, but that he loved us and sent his Son to be the means by which our sins are forgiven (1 John 4:10).

● Thank God right now for his great love for you.

3 Superglue

Once we have given our lives to Jesus, he promises that *nothing* will ever be able to separate us from him – and he means *nothing*! Here is the promise he has given us:

I am certain that nothing can separate us from his love: neither death nor life, neither angels nor other heavenly rulers or powers, neither the present nor the future, neither the world above nor the world below – there is nothing in all creation that will ever be able to separate us from the love of God which is ours through Christ Jesus our Lord (Romans 8:38–39).

● Why not go to the window right now and shout 'Hallelujah' at the top of your voice, so that you can be heard right down the street! This is the best news in the world. Nothing can ever separate you from God's love. Nothing!

4 Daily bath

So what about things we still do wrong? How does God see them, and what does he do about them? The answer is simple – we have to have a daily bath. The Bible says:

If we say that we have no sin, we deceive ourselves, and there is no truth in us. But if we confess our sins to God, he will keep his promise and do what is right: he will forgive us our sins, and purify us from all our wrongdoing (1 John 1:8–9).

This means that at the end of every day we must stop and let the Holy Spirit remind us of the things that we have done wrong during that day. Then we confess them to Jesus and they are dealt with by him. If we don't take this daily bath, then we will feel that God is not as close to us as we would like. That's why daily confession is so essential to us. But remember, *nothing* can separate us from the love of God.

It may well be that sometimes the things that Jesus brings to mind are big things, and however much we say sorry we don't get a sense of forgiveness. When that happens it's good to find someone we can trust and share what's happening with them, so that together we can pray to God. Most Christians find from time to time that they need to confess their sins to God in the presence of another Christian. Make sure the person you choose is one you can really trust.

SORRY
● Think back.
● Confess.
● Believe you are forgiven.

WE'RE FORGIVEN
Remember that –
1 even our best actions are 'filthy through and through'. (See Isaiah 64:6.)
2 Jesus took the 'sin of the world' on himself. (See John 1:29.)
3 we are made 'clean as snow'. (See Isaiah 1:18.)

THANK YOU
Spend some time each day thanking God for his great love for you – a love so great that he had made it possible for you to be forgiven and to become one of his people.

God's way

Violence

LINK: Forgiving – a DIY guide (page 52)
Loving – a way of life (page 30)

Some months ago one of my son's friends brought a video to our house. When I found out that it was *Kung Fu Fighter* I wouldn't let them see it, because I'm not happy about violent films. Off they went (probably to watch it on somebody else's video!) and I sat down to watch the news on TV.

The news was all about:
● a bomb explosion in Northern Ireland, with some appalling pictures of the victims.
● a story about a man convicted of murder, with descriptions of exactly what he had done.
● details of the increase in child abuse in Britain, with some examples.

That was the national news. When the regional programme came on it was more of the same – rapes, muggings, robberies and so on.

Violence is everywhere

Violence surrounds us – on the TV or radio, in the papers, in our streets, sometimes even in our homes – and it affects us all. Some of the areas where it comes up are:
● war. (See 'War', page 46.) This is a regular news item for all to see. There are small wars and big ones, but in all of them people are killed, injured, damaged. We get so used to seeing it that sometimes we stop responding to how terrible it is.
● muggings and violent crime. All age groups are at risk from this kind of violence. Some readers of this book will have been victims, or know people who have been victims. A few readers may have been involved in committing crime.
● bullying, threatening behaviour and fighting. Every school has its bullies. Many live in fear of being bullied by them and even threatened with violence if they do not toe the line. Threats hurt, and it's only a short step from threat to action.
● TV, video, films, newspapers and books. Some people have committed violent crimes because of what they have seen on TV. It's all too easy to become what we see or read about.
● in the home. There's a lot of violence in many homes – either actual or threatened. Some readers may have been hit, hurt or even raped or abused at home.

Christians cannot hide from these facts of life. How does God expect us to live in our violent society? There's no easy answer, but here are a few suggestions to think and pray about.

1 Be peaceful!
The source of violence is inside people – and not just other people but us too! It begins when we feel anger, resentment, jealousy, bitterness, selfishness,

a desire to get even, to hurt because we have been hurt, or because we enjoy seeing others hurt. So it's essential that:

- Jesus is our Lord (see 'Knowing Jesus for yourself', page 4). If we haven't given control of our lives to Jesus then we've no defence against all the evil things that are inside of us.
- we are disciplined in our lives. We need to train ourselves **not** to be violent in our language, our behaviour, our relationships with others, our thoughts. (To make a start we need to think about what we read, listen to and watch.) Only the Holy Spirit can help us do this – ask him to show you and to help you right now.
- we take practical steps. I don't watch violent entertainment on TV, and I switch it off or change the channel when violence begins to appear. When violent scenes appear on the news I start to pray. I don't read violent books and I don't buy newspapers that give grisly details of violence as a means of selling the paper. These are my personal decisions – what are yours going to be?

I'm trying to let God control my violent reactions. I used to have a very quick temper. It still flares occasionally, but with God's help I'm getting it under control. At least I know the danger – do you know your flash points? I can also say the nastiest things, and sometimes in very bad language. I haven't made much progress in this area, but at least I know it's an area that needs prayer. What are your prayer areas?

2 Work for peace
Violence is one of Satan's strongholds, and only prayer can break it down. So could you:
- encourage your youth fellowship or school CU to begin a prayer group to pray for peace in your area and in the world?

Don't be fooled by Satan. Prayer is the one thing he fears above all else, and prayer is the one thing that really can defeat violence and bring about change. Don't be discouraged – get praying.

LOOK INTO THE BIBLE
Look up –
- Matthew 18:21–35 on forgiveness.
- Isaiah 53:1–9 on non-violence.
- Isaiah 53:10–12 on what non-violence can achieve.
- Proverbs 15:1 on how to react to provocation.

3 Don't get used to it
We see so much violence, that we can become almost used to it. Fight against this feeling. Ask God to let you always feel the horror of it.

4 Be concerned
Victims of violence need prayer, support and encouragement. Do you know anyone you can befriend? Why not find out about

CARE (write to CARE Trust, 57 Romney Street, London SW1P 3RF) or get involved in a victim support group of some sort. Ask at your local library or Citizens Advice Bureau for where to find such groups in your area.

5 Know forgiveness
Maybe you have been involved in violence yourself and have hurt others. It's not always easy to live with the guilt that this brings – the TV never tells you about this. But God is a forgiving God (see 'Forgiveness – God's way', page 40). No matter what you have done he wants to forgive you and set you free from guilt. Why not:
- ask for his forgiveness right now.
- find a Christian friend that you can talk things over with.
- do now what God tells you.

Here is a prayer for forgiveness: 'Lord I've hurt someone. I'm so ashamed, and truly sorry. Please forgive me. Help them to forgive me. Show me if there is anything I can do to heal the hurt. Help me to remember that Jesus' death takes away every sin. Amen.'

When I was making the packed lunches before school the other day I went to get out the Kit Kats. There should have been three in the cupboard – but there were none! Everyone denied touching them – even though it was obvious that someone was guilty. So why didn't anyone own up?

The reason is plain – no one wanted to get into trouble! Being truthful sounds good in theory, but when it comes to the crunch we soon realise that living by the truth can lead to tough situations.

LINK: Satan (page 16)

Living by the Truth

Jesus always lived by the truth. He made this claim about himself: "I am the way, the truth, and the life" (John 14:6) – and his life measured up to his claim.

- He spoke truth in the face of his enemies (John 5:19).
- He spoke it to those who believed in him (John 8:32).
- He spoke it to his closest followers (John 13:16).
- He spoke it to those who had the power to kill him (John 18:37).
- He spoke truth even when it meant being unpopular (John 6:66).
- He lived by it all the time (John 8:46).

Why did Jesus choose to live by the truth, no matter how difficult things got as a consequence? The answer is that Jesus was God, and since God is truth Jesus could not live any other way. We read that he was 'full of grace and truth' (John 1:14).

If we believe in Jesus then we've got to live by the truth too. No matter how hard it is there is no other way for us to live. Ask God to help you know what truth is and ask him to give you the courage to follow the path of truth.

Opposition!

The Bible tells us that Satan is the enemy of truth. In fact not only is he a liar, he is the father of lies (John 8:44). Jesus came to destroy the works of the devil (1 John 3:8) and he began by showing up the lies – by living the truth. If you believe in Jesus you are Satan's enemy, for he hates truth. So you can expect him to try and stop you:

- knowing what is truth,
- doing what is true,
- encouraging others to live by the truth.

Have you ever wondered why it is so hard to live by the truth, and how easy it is to live with lies? The answer is that you are fighting alongside Jesus against the father of lies. Ask God to help and strengthen you. Make sure you put on the heavenly armour (see Ephesians 6:14–17). (See also 'Satan', page 16.)

Going straight

To live by the truth, as Jesus shows and teaches, is the best way to live, however painful it may seem at the time. Lies might seem attractive, but they only lead to more lies. But living by the truth is hard and we have to take some action if we are going to do it.

2 Look out for the truth

It isn't always easy knowing what is truth and what is not truth. There are many complicated issues to face in our modern world. So we have to think, pray, read the Bible and listen to others, if we are going to get the truth right. It's an effort, and it's much easier not to bother. Are you prepared to make the effort?

3 Stand up for the truth

On some occasions we will find that we believe something is right because God says it, but others will disagree. Then we can be very uncomfortable – it isn't easy being the odd one out. But our job is to stand up for the truth whatever the cost, just as Christ did. Ask God to give you the strength to stand for the truth.

1 Get rid of lies

If there are any parts of your life that are built on lies, then putting them right will lead you into truth. Are there things you are ashamed of, things that need confessing and putting right? Then ask God to help you do so (see 'Forgiveness – God's way', page 40).

- **Knowing what's true.** Is your life built on the foundation of truth? For example, do you know God's truth on sex, love, behaviour, etc?
- **Speaking the truth.** Do you:
  – always speak it?
  – occasionally speak it?
  – not speak it when it will get you into trouble?
  – tell white lies?
  – keep quiet when you feel like it?
  How are you going to make sure you always tell the truth?
- **Standing up for truth.** When your friends disagree do you:
  – put a case for what the Bible says?
  – agree to compromise a little?
  – keep quiet, because it's easier?
  Standing for the truth can be very painful, especially with your friends. They might stop going around with you. Are you prepared for this?

LOOK INTO THE BIBLE

Living by the truth can get us into hot water, but it can also bring us through bad times into God's place for us. Joseph's life in Egypt is a good example of this. See Genesis 39–41. Joseph found that living by the truth brought trouble – see Genesis 39. Does chapter 41 show a different side to telling the truth? See Genesis 41:39–41 – does telling the truth always end up in this sort of way?

4 Enjoy the truth

If we believe in the truth and stand for it we are safe, because we are standing on the rock of God's truth. Read this:

Whoever goes to the Lord for safety,
whoever remains under the protection of the Almighty,
can say to him,
"You are my defender and protector.
You are my God; in you I trust"
(Psalm 91:1–2).

Spend a few moments reading this and enjoying the safety that the truth gives to you.

WAR

LINK: Violence (page 42)

How big is your world? Home, school, where you live, where you go on holiday? Sorry, but the world is a much bigger place than this! Too often we make the mistake of thinking all that matters is our own little patch and what we are doing in it.

Jesus had wider horizons. He said: "Heaven and earth will pass away, but my words will never pass away" (Luke 21:33). And he encouraged his disciples to widen their horizons as well.

"I have been given all authority in heaven and earth. Go, then, to all peoples everywhere and make them my disciples" (Matthew 28:18).

Our faith in Jesus is to do with the whole world, not just how we live as a Christian at home and at school or work. So forget the homework, the telly, and the boy/girlfriend, and get thinking about war. Get an idea of the problem.
● How many wars are being fought today – can you list three of them?

● Think of some major conflict from the last few years. Do you know how many people were killed in it?
● How much nerve gas is being stored in the world at the moment?

Answers

● In the mid-1980s it was estimated that 40 wars of different sizes were being fought. The numbers keep changing but this gives you an idea of the size of the problem.
● One major conflict of the last few years was between Iran and Iraq. Nobody knows exactly how many people were killed, but it could be 700,000 or more. This takes some imagining. If your local comprehensive has 1000 students it means that 700 times that many people have been killed. Imagine how many grieving families that means. Many more will have been injured or maimed.
● It's been estimated that there is enough nerve gas around to kill each one of us 8000 times over. And that's just nerve gas!

Just as we can become used to violence (see page 42) so we can become used to war. With so much of it around it's easy almost to ignore it, especially when other things claim our attention. It may be hard to get stirred up about things that happen far away but we must be concerned with world issues or we are denying Christ's authority over all his creation.

'But what can I do about war?' you ask. Christians have been trying to sort out answers to this question for a long time. Sometimes Christians disagree. I'm not going to look at all the arguments but will concentrate on the things we all agree about and the practical steps we can take.

1 War is evil
No matter how good the cause and whatever the outcome, war is an evil thing. God didn't intend that it should afflict people's lives. Jesus gave this command: "Live in peace with one another" (Mark 9:50). That's good advice for individuals and nations.

2 Talking is better than fighting
However long negotiations take it's better to make progress by talking, even with regimes and countries we don't agree with, rather than start a war where many people will suffer on both sides.

3 Leaders need prayer
In the end, it's the nations' leaders who decide on war. Christians should be praying for them by name regularly and intelligently (see 1 Timothy 2:2). Stop and make a list now of major world leaders. Then do your homework over the next week and add some more names to your list! It's vital that we keep up to date on what's happening in the world, so try to find out who's who and what they're doing.

4 Encourage peace
Sometimes leaders need to be reminded of ordinary people's desire for peace. This can strengthen those who do everything possible to avoid war.

5 War – the only way?
It seems that there are times when there is no alternative but to go to war. Justice demands it. But even as a last resort, is it the only way? What do you think?

6 Healing must come
When wars are over, there's a need for healing of the damage to shattered lives and the destruction of the environment. People need care and loving attention, and trust and co-operation between nations has to be rebuilt. There's a part for all Christians to play in this healing process.

Just as Satan wants to stop us praying against violence, so he wants us to give up bothering about war. He wants us to think that we're too insignificant, and that we cannot make any difference.

ACTION
1 Pray about a particular war. It's hard to pray for all war troubled countries, so pick one and keep that in your prayers. Keep up to date with what is happening.
2 Write to the leaders of the countries involved. Leaders need to know what you feel. Ask leaders what they are doing for peace, why they are fighting, and when they are planning to stop. I know it looks a small thing to do, but who knows what God can do through your letter?
3 Support the United Nations. It's the best thing we have to get warring nations at least talking. Take an interest in what they do and pray for peace.
4 Keep your church informed. Make sure others in your church, youth group or CU are kept informed about what's happening in the part of the world you're praying about. Spread the news — war is bad news.

Money
LINK: Third world issues (page 78)
Loving – a way of life (page 30)

&Materialism

Maybe your problem is that you haven't enough money to buy all the things you want! Or perhaps you've got an even bigger problem? You look at all the things your friends spend money on – the latest fashion clothes and accessories, Walkmans, make-up, tapes, records, hair dos, chips – and then see pictures of starving people in Ethiopia and other parts of the world and feel guilty, wondering just what God makes of it.

To start looking at how God sees money and possessions:
● Make a list of *ten* things you own, noting alongside each one how much it is worth.
● Make a list of *five* things you want, noting how much each will cost.

Think positive

I often have to use this heading when writing and speaking about God. That's because we are so quick to think that God is a negative person – always ready to tell us what not to do and frowning on us when we happen to enjoy something. But it's quite the opposite – God is very positive and is always looking for opportunities to encourage us, and to help us enjoy his world. Of course he occasionally has to be firm with us and say 'no' or 'no more', but that's much less common than we expect. To help us enjoy his world he's given us a code to live by. What does it say about money and things?
● Everything we have is a gift from him, including our money and possessions. The Bible tells us

Every good gift . . . comes down from heaven; it comes down from God (James 1:17).

● There is nothing evil about money. It's one of the gifts God has given us. He warns us, though, 'the love of money is a source of all kinds of evil' (1 Timothy 6:10).

LOOK INTO THE BIBLE
Read –
● the story of the rich fool in Luke 12:13–21.
● the story of the sower in Mark 4:1–20.
● about Christian giving in 2 Corinthians 9.

Look at you!

Have you got it wrong about money and the way you use it? Stop now and thank God for all the good things he has given you – including money and possessions.

What's the problem?

Along with the thankfulness for money and possessions has to come an awareness of the dangers. If you ignore these then you cannot hope to please God. The main problems are:

● lovely money. The problems come when we fall in love with money. It can get a hold of us, almost like a drug, until we want more and more of it. Becoming a 'moneyaholic' will spoil your friendship with God and with other people. Ask yourself: has money got a stranglehold on you?

● lovely things. Possessions can become too important to us. Jesus told a parable about a man who had this problem. He had a bumper harvest in his fields, but instead of being thankful to God, he said,

'I haven't anywhere to keep all my crops. What can I do? . . . . I will tear down my barns and build bigger ones, where I will store all my corn and all my other goods. Then I will say to myself, Lucky man! You have all the good things you need for many years. Take life easy, eat, drink and enjoy yourself!' But God said to him, 'You fool! This very night you will have to give up your life; then who will get all these things you have kept for yourself?' (Luke 12:16–20.)

When possessions and money become more important to us than God's love, then we're in trouble.

What can I do to get it right?

There's no need to get all tangled up over money and possessions, as long as we look to God for guidance. Try these practical steps to get things right.

1 You are God's banker. Try seeing your money not as your own, but as God's money, left in your keeping. Ask his advice before you spend. Where does your money go at the moment? From now on, keep a list of what you buy and look over it regularly asking, 'Is God happy about it all?'

2 Give God his share. God expects some return on the money he has trusted you with. It can be given to him through offering at church, or by giving to support some Christian work. You may do this already. But how generous are you? Take a look at Malachi 3:6–12 and Leviticus 27:30–34, then think about the way you give to God.

The Bible gives us a guideline of giving at least ten per cent of our money back to God in this way. That works out at 10p for every £1.00 we have. Perhaps half of what we give could go to help feed hungry people through a Christian agency like TEAR Fund, and the rest to God's work through your church.

3 Give God the final say. Look at the list that you made earlier of things you want to get. Talk about each one with God. Be willing to take some time over it. Don't be totally persuaded by TV ads or friends. Let God have some say in how you spend his money.

THANK YOU

Spend a little time thanking God for all you have. There's nothing worse than being ungrateful.

ACTION NOW

If money or possessions have got a hold over you –

● tell God about it right now.

● ask for his Holy Spirit to help you know what to do.

● ask God for a new way of living with money and possessions.

● do what he tells you.

F·A·C·I·N·G
EVIL

LINK: Satan (page 16)

In the next few sections we're going to look at some of the difficult issues that face us today – areas where evil has a very powerful grip. As Christians we are challenged by Christ to get involved in the world, and we're going to have to work out how to do this. But before we do that let's get hold of some basic steps in facing evil.

1 Know the enemy

The first thing is to know the enemy. (See 1 Peter 5:8.) The Bible tells us all we need to know about him. (See 'Satan', page 16.) It's important to expect Satan to be against everything that is good – it'll help keep us praying.

2 Know the power of the cross

We can share in Jesus' victory over Satan and all his works, because of what Jesus has done on the cross. Read these verses:

On that cross Christ freed himself from the power of the spiritual rulers and authorities; he made a public spectacle of them by leading them as captives in his victory procession (Colossians 2:15).

. . . so that through his death he (Jesus) might destroy the Devil, who has the power over death, and in this way set free those who were slaves all their lives because of their fear of death (Hebrews 2:14–15).

One of Satan's favourite techniques is to make us feel defeated. How often have you said about a major problem, 'It's impossible'? Remember that we share in Jesus' victory.

● Pause now. Read again the verses above and ask the Holy Spirit to let you know and feel the power of Christ's victory.

Facing evil can mean going a different way to everyone else.

3 Know the power of forgiveness

There is nothing that anyone can do which cannot be forgiven, because of the death of Jesus on the cross. As we look at areas where evil seems to be so strong this fact has to be remembered again and again. Jesus can forgive any sin – absolutely any sin. This is another truth which Satan doesn't want us to believe. Learn this verse – it will help you remember the completeness of Christ's forgiveness:

He loves us, and by his death he has freed us from our sins (Revelation 1:5).

4 Know the Bible

The Bible is our great weapon against evil and also our great defence against mistaking evil for good. (See Ephesians 6:17.) We need to know it, read it, pray with it and trust it. When Jesus was under the attack of Satan (see Luke 4:1–13) he defeated evil by quoting three times from the Old Testament. Satan had no answer to him. We must learn the same lesson.

● Pause now. Are you reading the Bible regularly? Ask God to give you the desire to do so.

5 Know the power of prayer

Steady persistent prayer can overcome evil – it's like the sea wearing down the sea shore. Sometimes we see great successes – at other times it's just the steady day by day, year by year, decade by decade prayer that does the job. Sometimes we are tempted to give up when we don't see instant results (that's just another trick of the enemy to deflect us). Have a look at Mark 9:14–29.

● Pause now. Ask God for a deeper desire to pray.

6 Be discerning

Do not restrain the Holy Spirit; do not despise inspired messages. Put all things to the test: keep what is good, and avoid every kind of evil (1 Thessalonians 5:19–22).

When dealing with evil things it's vital that we put everything to the test before the Lord. These are the sorts of things we should be asking:

● 'Lord, what is evil here?'
● 'Lord, lead me to the right part of your word to help me.'
● 'Lord, help me to know what to do.'
● 'Lord, help me to pray until I know what is right.'
● 'Lord, lead me to anyone or anything that can help me know what to do.'

There are two extremes for Christians to fall into when dealing with evil – we either fail to see it at all or we see Satan in absolutely everything that happens. We need to be discerning so that we can avoid either trap and, with God's help, keep a balanced view of evil.

ACTION WATCH

● What evil activities do you feel you should be praying against?
● Are there others who can join you?

● Are you falling asleep on watch? Satan loves sleepy Christians — people who aren't aware of what he is doing because they can't be bothered to make the effort to find out.

Forgiving –

LINK: Sex (page 54)
Rape (page 56)
Abuse (page 58)
Homosexuality (page 60)

The heart of the Christian faith is knowing that we are forgiven through the death of Jesus. Because of him we can lead new lives. But forgiveness is a more complicated issue than we sometimes think.

Forgiveness covers, for example:
• knowing that we need forgiveness from God, asking for it, and knowing that we have received it.
• asking forgiveness from others, if we have hurt them.
• giving forgiveness to others if they have hurt us.
• forgiving freely, without having a feeling of resentment.
• living with those who cannot yet forgive us.

This is a tough area for us. Peter, Jesus' disciple, thought he had a formula for getting things straight when he asked, "Lord, if my brother keeps on sinning against me, how many times do I have to forgive him? Seven times?" "No, not seven times," answered Jesus, "but seventy times seven" (Matthew 18:21–22).

Jesus wasn't expecting Peter to carry a calculator around with him so that once he reached seventy times seven he could stop forgiving! The point he was trying to make was that forgiving others is something we are going to have to get used to, if we want to be Jesus' followers. It needs to become a way of life for us – that's why it's included in the Lord's prayer: 'Forgive us the wrongs we have done, as we forgive the wrongs that others have done to us' (Matthew 6:12).

All very nice in theory, isn't it, but in practice we find forgiveness a very hard issue.

Have you ever used any of these excuses?
• 'Why should I forgive him? It was his fault not mine.'
• 'If I say "sorry" he will think that I am weak and will do all he can to hurt me.'
• 'If I say "sorry" I will look small in the eyes of my friends.'
• 'I can always say "sorry" later.'
• 'I've said "sorry" enough times already to him – I'm not saying it again.'

Maybe we can manage forgiveness about 'little' things, but how do we forgive someone who's done something very terrible? Working out the principles of forgiveness in these areas of life is far from easy. But we've still got to learn to forgive – and to do it in the real hard world, where really big problems – like abuse, rape, violence and evil – are around. Where can we start?

1 God forgives us
Before we even consider forgiving others, it's good to remember just how much we need forgiveness from God for ourselves. How many things has God had to forgive you for today? This week? This month? Do you realise that if we sin just three times a day, every day, God is having to forgive us over a thousand times a year – and it's probably lots more than that anyway. God loves us so much,

A DIY GUIDE

that he is prepared to go on forgiving and forgiving. (See 1 John 1:8–9.) Isn't this a good starting point for forgiving others?

2 We forgive our family

If God has forgiven us, then we must forgive others and the starting point is inside our family where forgiveness is hardest. How easy do you find it to forgive your parents – and to ask for their forgiveness when you know you have been in the wrong? (Have a look at Exodus 20:12.) How easy is it to forgive your brother, sister, aunt or uncle? How easy is it to confess to them that you have been wrong, and to ask forgiveness from them? If we cannot forgive those inside our family we are going to find it hard to forgive those who are outside it.

It's important to let God set the pace in this matter. As we keep close to him in our prayers, he will make it clear who he wants us to forgive or ask for forgiveness. And he will show us when the right moment comes along.

3 We forgive our spiritual family

Next in line for forgiveness are those members of our spiritual family – our brothers and sisters in Christ. Are there people in church or your Christian group that you resent or despise? Are there people whom you know that you have hurt? Are there

people in your fellowship who have hurt you? Are you willing to offer them unconditional forgiveness? It's often hard to do this, and only the Holy Spirit working in your life can see you through. Ask the Spirit right now to give you the strength to forgive – and take a look at Luke 11:4.

4 We forgive those who hurt us

It's really tough to forgive those who hurt us and go on doing it with no intention of stopping. It's really hard to forgive those who hurt us very badly – abuse us, physically violate us, emotionally harass and crush us – and then either get away with it, or come and ask forgiveness. Jesus must have felt this as he was nailed to the cross, yet he cried out, "Forgive them, Father, they don't know what they are doing." This is the quality of forgiveness he asks of us. (See Matthew 5:44.) It isn't easy, but it does make us more like him. This is the quality of forgiveness which will reach people who seem so against Jesus.

GET PRAYING

● A prayer to help us forgive:
'Father, I know that you have forgiven me. But I find it so hard to forgive others. Please fill me with your Holy Spirit. Show me who to forgive. Show me how to forgive. Give me the courage to forgive.'

● A prayer for those who need forgiveness:
'Father, I have wronged another person. I need to ask for their forgiveness right now, but I haven't the courage. Please help me. Give me the desire and the opportunity to ask forgiveness. I cannot do it without your help.'

● A prayer to use if you've been badly hurt:
'Father, you know how badly I have been hurt. It's so very hard to forgive the one who has hurt me. But I know that this is what you want. Please help me to forgive.'

Sex

LINK: Boy meets girl . . . (page 32)

I've just had a letter from a teenager telling me that she and her boyfriend have been having sexual intercourse. They've realised that this is wrong and so they've decided to stick with heavy petting – right through to orgasm – when they feel like it. 'After all', the letter goes on, 'we both love each other and this gives us such pleasure. Surely it's not wrong, is it? We've talked to our friends, and they all agree that what we're doing is OK.'

Like so many young people today this couple are struggling to get their thinking straight. But thinking straight is difficult when there's so much encouragement to misuse our sexuality. Newspapers carry pictures of naked women and stories of rape: most newsagents openly sell pornographic material. Most video shops are the same – only worse! It's so easy to think that anything goes, as long as boy and girl agree. So how can we manage to live as God wants? And what does God want anyway?

Don't be taken in!

It's very important to recognise that we are living in a time of great confusion about sex and that there are those who are out to exploit our sexual feelings for their own ends. Sex sells things, and so people use this device to increase their profits – and care little about morality. Don't be conned by them.

It's fun!

It's fun being with the opposite sex. God made things that way – not just because through sexual intercourse we can have children but because he knows that being together can make for a full and satisfying experience of life. And there's loads we can do together which doesn't have to result in sexual activity like petting or intercourse.

Intimate sex is for marriage

Read this:

Jesus said . . . . "In the beginning, at the time of creation, 'God made them male and female,' as the scripture says. 'And for this reason a man will leave his father and mother and unite with his wife, and the two will become one'" (Mark 10:5–9).

Men and women were made for each other – and intimate sexual experience is meant to be kept inside the marriage relationship. Once we break this pattern and have sex outside of a permanent, fully committed relationship with one other person then it becomes nothing more than a cheap experience. Sex outside marriage often brings with it many emotional problems – guilt and feelings of shame. People who have sex outside marriage should also think about genito-urinary infections and even AIDS.

• The pressure is on to have sex and not to wait for marriage. How do you feel about this?

Once we can get hold of these principles, then some of the other questions become clearer. Ask yourself, for example:

• Do dirty jokes, gossip about sex, or pornography help me in my relationships with the opposite sex? If they don't then they need to stop. This could mean saying, 'I don't want to hear about . . .' or even walking away from people doing these things. But that could lead to your being thrown out of your group. How do you feel about this?

• Does 'Everyone's doing it' make it right? Because some of your friends are having sex, should you do the same? It's hard to stand out against the crowd: you can feel very lonely. Are you prepared to pay this kind of price? (Don't forget, when it comes to boasting about sexual exploits, some of your friends may be exaggerating or even lying. Maybe you should be feeling sorry for them, not worrying about 'catching up'.)

• Masturbation can be difficult to decide about. Maybe we should be asking, 'Is it making me a better person?' The physical act of masturbation isn't wrong – but the thoughts that can go with it may be, and they spoil us as people. And it can leave a feeling of guilt which is never a good thing.

How should I live?

1 Be confident in yourself
Read this: 'Then God said "And now we will make human beings; they will be like us and resemble us"' (Genesis 1:26). We are valuable to God for who we are, not for what we do. So if someone starts to ridicule you about your lack of sexual experience or your unwillingness to have sex, calling you frigid, or inexperienced – don't feel beaten down. God loves you for who you are, not for your sexual experience (or lack of it).

2 Be on guard
We need to watch out, so that the world's attitudes don't become ours. Ask God to examine your motives every day, and he will root out that which doesn't come from him. Have a look at Psalm 139:23–24.

3 Stand firm
Sexual attitudes are to do with what we think, what we look at and what we do. Ask God to control these areas of your life. To be disciplined and strong in sexual matters is not weakness, but real strength, and it comes from God. Keeping yourself for your future husband or wife is part of God's plan. To be a virgin on your wedding night is what the world calls stupid. But don't believe it! The opposite is true. God made us and he knows what's best for us – so believe his word.

LOOK INTO THE BIBLE
The Bible contains some sorry stories about the misuse of sex. Read about David and Bathsheba in 2 Samuel 11, or about Tamar in 2 Samuel 13. Remember that God can forgive all sin – and that includes sexual sin. See John 8:1–11.

RAPE

LINK: Sex (page 54)

Rape – the crime of having sex with a woman against her will – is a very serious offence.

Facts and feelings

Rape is not a new crime. Men have always wanted women whom they could not have, and have taken them by force. (See 2 Samuel 13.) What some people (particularly men?) don't always realise is just how violent the crime is and how it devastates – sometimes beyond repair – the lives of the women who are the victims.

One woman recently spoke to a national magazine about how she had been raped and said, 'I ate and ate to make myself fat and unattractive to men, until I realised that rape had as much to do with power over women as it did with sex. It's been very hard, but I'm determined not to be a permanent victim of what happened.'

Another woman, speaking very courageously in JAM magazine, said, 'My friends were stunned . . . at first they didn't know whether to mention the rape or not. It was usually me that broke the ice. But they were there when I needed them. Acquaintances treated me as though I had developed a deformity. At first I became distant with my father. The event put a lot of strain on all our family relationships, and it wasn't helped by the fact that we couldn't discuss what had happened because of legal reasons.

But it was through talking and more talking that I've been helped very slowly. My friends have been great. I still don't feel comfortable with most men when I'm on my own in a confined area. And I find it hard when people I don't know very well are talking about rape. I've forgiven the men involved. I hate what happened, but I don't hate them.

The seriousness of rape cannot be too strongly emphasised. It's a terrible crime which leaves women deeply – and often permanently – hurt.

Christian men – read this!

Read Psalm 24:3–4 and Matthew 5:27–28. Think about it.
● Women are objects of lust to a lot of men. It's hard to resist thinking the same way – particularly when there is so much pornography and exploitation around. But it's important to win the battle in our minds, and think of women as people, not things. It's important, too, to gain control over our eyes – otherwise we are, in effect, raping the women around us. Jesus said, "Anyone who looks at a woman and wants to possess her is guilty of committing adultery with her in his heart" (Matthew 5:28).

- Women are people, made in the image of God. We must get into the habit of treating them like this – learning to appreciate everything that God has made them to be, not just noticing their sexual characteristics.
- Our attitudes to women are shaped by what we read and watch. Beware of newspapers which carry sensational stories about rape or indecent assault, or which feature nudes. Pornographic magazines are definitely out! Watch out also for videos and TV programmes which feature pornographic material or which glorify violence towards women. Jesus said, "The mouth speaks what the heart is full of" (Luke 6.45). Make sure it isn't full of filth!

We're all involved!

- Sexual instincts are very strong and, if uncontrolled, lead to great sorrow. Amnon raped Tamar (see 2 Samuel 13) and Potiphar's wife wanted to sleep with Joseph (see Genesis 39) because they wouldn't control their feelings. (Used rightly, our sexual instincts can lead to a happy relationship of mutual trust and care – with neither partner exercising power over the other.) Surrender all your feelings to God and ask him to help you control them.
- We need to challenge the attitudes to women in our society, because rape grows out of these twisted attitudes. At school – avoid making sexual remarks and don't listen to others who make them. At home – don't read the obscene papers, or watch obscene TV. At the shops – don't spend your money at shops that sell pornography, and encourage others to do the same.
- Help those who have been raped. Often women won't go to the police but they will tell their closest friends. We have to be caring and very sensitive as we try to help heal the hurts and re-establish a sense of worth, value and wholeness. (If you've a friend who needs this kind of

support, why not visit one of the groups listed in the HELP box?) We know that Jesus can help in this. One woman who had been raped said: 'Christian songs have really spoken to me over the last year. God has made me new – the pain is still there, but I'm a new person. I prayed a lot about how I felt, because I knew God was the only person who could really understand. I have never asked him why it happened to me; I just said, "OK, give me the strength to go on." I think I've grown a lot closer to him and learnt to trust more. Just knowing he loves me where I'm at – that keeps me going.'

Abuse

LINK: Forgiving — a DIY guide (page 5

This is another area where Christians have got to get their thinking clear. More and more cases of abuse, and in particular sexual abuse of children and young people, are coming to light. Some people reading this will have been abused as children, or will know those who have been abused.

The facts

The facts are very unpleasant, but it's important to understand them.

1 Sexual abuse

This is defined by the NSPCC as being where 'children (girls and boys) are sexually abused by adults who use them to meet their own sexual needs. This might be sexual intercourse, and also includes fondling, masturbation, oral sex, anal intercourse, and exposing children to pornographic material, including videos.'

Sexual abuse has long-term consequences, as it did for Mandy (not her real name), whose natural father sexually abused her for ten years before the family was referred to the NSPCC. The abuse began when she was four, and came to light only when she was fourteen. Three younger children in the family were also physically abused. For Mandy the trauma of her abuse was not over when the problem was revealed. Her profound sense of guilt and shame were compounded by the need to make repeated statements.

2 Physical abuse

This is when 'parents physically hurt, injure or kill a child. This can involve hitting, shaking, squeezing, burning and biting. It also includes giving a child poisonous substances, inappropriate drugs and alcohol, and attempted suffocating and drowning.'

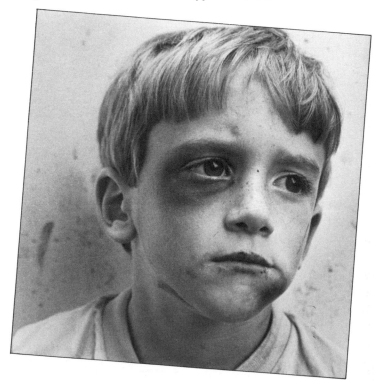

In most cases the NSPCC have found that someone in the family carries out the abuse. Thousands of children are abused every year, four out of five being girls. Many are too scarred to report the abuse, and are seriously damaged mentally by what happens to them.

Things to think about

This is a very difficult and painful issue, and there are no easy answers. But the Bible gives us some guidelines.

- Abuse is wrong (see Exodus 20:1–17). All forms of abuse, violence and hurt are against God's clear command. Again and again Jesus underlined this truth – by his love, his concern and his care for all of God's creatures. We need to hold on to this truth in a world gone wrong, where violence and pain are seen regularly on TV and in the papers, and where some even seem to glorify violence.
- The abused need healing (see John 8:2–11). Those who have been abused need to know the healing love of God. It's easy to write this and easy to believe it. But it's not so easy to put into practice, because those who have been abused don't easily talk about it. How is Mandy going to find God's healing touch?
- The abusers need healing. Those who have committed these crimes need to know the forgiveness of God (see 'Forgiveness – God's way', page 40). They need to know the forgiveness of those they have hurt, and a chance to begin a new life, free from their past failures. This is the message of the cross, but society is often not so forgiving, or understanding. Again it's easy to write this, but if you've been abused, it's a hard thing to consider.

What can we do?

1 Break the chain of violence

We need to control our aggressive feelings, our actions and our words. There must be no trace of violence or aggression in our lives, so that we're not passing on violent attitudes and behaviour to our friends, or in time to our children. In this way, we begin to break the chain of violence.

- Do you have a non-violent attitude? Look again at Luke 6:27–36.

2 Attitudes need to be challenged

The social attitudes towards abuse – those abused and those who abuse – need to be healing and forgiving. It's not that we condone what has happened, but we're trying to encourage people to move on from what's happened, to a position where they can be helped, healed and forgiven. This needs to be our attitude – is it yours?

3 Help those who are hurt

Do you have a friend who has been abused? Do you feel you don't know how to help? There are some things that you can do without making things worse.

- *Listen.* We need to talk to people about our hurts, and if your friend wants to talk to you, make sure you're available. This is a great gift to offer your friend.
- *Resist advising.* It's so easy to give advice, but often our friends don't need it – they just need to know that you're there, listening.
- *Show you love them.* People who have been abused sometimes feel valueless, that no one loves or cares about them. Try to show that you care, when opportunities come up naturally.
- *Keep confidences.* Don't tell others what your friend is saying to you – keep it between you, them and God.

ACTION

Support the agencies that are tackling abuse. They produce good informative literature, and offer counselling and help to anyone that needs it. Contact the National Society for the Prevention of Cruelty to Children, 67 Saffron Hill, London EC1N 8RS or Childline, Freepost 1111, London EC4B 4BB, Freephone 0800 1111.

HOMOSEXUALITY

This is another hot issue for Christians. Society seems confused or apathetic about this issue, and the church offers condemnation of homosexuality on the one hand, and the 'gay' Christian movement on the other.

Facts

Homosexuality is the emotional and sexual attraction of one person towards another of the same sex. (*Homo* means same.) It can be used to refer to both men and women, although lesbianism is the word often used to refer to female homosexuality. It has been said that three in ten men have had some type of homosexual experience at some point in their lives. The statistics for women are said to be slightly lower, although it is obviously difficult to know for sure.

Think about it

The Bible gives us a clear background to understand what our attitude to homosexuality should be.

God is love

It's only when we love God that we feel right about ourselves. Once we are open to God's love we feel whole people, with a place and a purpose here on earth and an eternal home in heaven. Because we are secure in God's love, and know we matter to him, we can start to work out a right attitude to sex. Read 1 John 4:7–11 and thank God for his goodness towards you and his love for you. Ask him to show you his love again today.

Sex: a problem area!

Getting the sexual balance in our lives is not easy for us (see 'Boy meets girl', page 32. Remember that God has as much – if not more – to say about lust, adultery, rape and abuse as he does about homosexuality. This at least helps us get things in perspective. We can be quick to condemn homosexual acts while being involved in lust, pornography and indecency. Do you have a critical spirit towards others, without noticing your own faults? (See Matthew 7:1–5.)

Sex is for marriage

Jesus put it like this:

"In the beginning, at the time of creation, 'God made them male and female,' as the scripture says. 'And for this reason a man will leave his father and mother and unite with his wife, and the two will become one.'" (Mark 10:6–7).

Intimate sexual relations are intended by God to be between a man and a woman, within a marriage. This is why rape, adultery and homosexual acts are outside of his plan. Have you had sex outside marriage? Then you are in as much need of forgiveness as someone guilty of a different sexual sin.

Homosexuality is spoken against

The passages of the Bible which refer to homosexuality need to be studied in a loving and concerned way. We should be wanting to love people and to help them discover God's best for their lives – not looking for an excuse to hurt them.
- Leviticus 18:22 – God condemns male homosexual acts.
- Romans 1:24–28 – homosexual activity is tied up with abandoning God's guidelines for life.

▲ *Homosexuality is a subject that makes for a heated debate!*

- 1 Corinthians 6:9–11 – homosexual acts are not okay in God's kingdom.

It takes courage to support what the Bible says. Do you?

God can forgive

The Bible tells us that God can change a person's feelings and behaviour, through the power of the Holy Spirit. Sometimes he uses personal difficulties – like struggling to do what's right about sex – as a source of Christian growth. Healing, in its widest sense, may take all these forms (see 2 Corinthians 1:3–7 and 12:9–10).

Forgiveness is at the heart of the Christian faith. God can forgive the sins of homosexual acts, just as he can forgive any sin. Do you need to know his forgiveness now? Then turn to the section on forgiveness (page 40) and get things sorted out. He guarantees to forgive you and to help you live a new life. Ask him to show you what he wants you to do now – and do it. It would be good to talk to a Christian friend, if you know one that you can trust.

ACTION

There are a number of organisations that can help you if you have been involved in homosexual relationships or if you just want to be better informed. I can recommend:
- True Freedom Trust, PO Box 3, Upton, Wirral, Merseyside L49 6NY. Phone 051 653 0773.

Their director, Martin Hallett, has written a very helpful book on this subject – *I am learning to love*, published by Marshall Pickering.
- Turnabout (London area), PO Box 592, London SE4 1EF. Phone 01 460 2425.

dRUgS

Facts

Most people are aware that drugs are very dangerous. Things ranging from heroin, cocaine, amphetamines and LSD to cannabis, solvents and tranquillisers have powerful addictive qualities and can – in the end – kill people. (One drug in particular – alcohol – is so widely used that it gets special treatment: see pages 66 and 67.) As most people know the dangers of misusing drugs, why does it still happen? Here are some of the reasons.
- *Need for acceptance.* We all like to feel we belong – that we're 'one of the gang'. Sometimes people get into groups where drug taking is part of the culture, and in these circumstances it's difficult *not* to take drugs. There's always the fear that to reject the drug will lead to being rejected by the group.
- *Need for experience.* Everyone likes a bit of excitement – and we're curious to find out why our friends like what they do! Life can seem dull, and we long for something more exciting. Some drugs bring a 'high', which promises a great experience.
- *Need to escape.* People can feel trapped in their circumstances (like family problems, or unemployment) and long for something better. They

believe that drugs will provide something better – and help them forget.

Think about it

The misuse of drugs is wrong
Read these verses:

Surely you know that you are God's temple and that God's Spirit lives in you! So if anyone destroys God's temple, God will destroy him. For God's temple is holy, and you yourselves are his temple
(1 Corinthians 3:16–17).

Drugs destroy us as people – destroy us physically, emotionally and spiritually. To damage our bodies in this or any other way is definitely outside God's will and purpose for us. Do you see the wrong in drugs, or do you compromise with your friends? How do you treat a friend who is taking drugs?

Who wins?
Read this verse:

For the love of money is a source of all kinds of evil
(1 Timothy 6:10).

Illegal drugs are a big money business – that's one of the reasons why it flourishes despite all the efforts to destroy it. For the love of money, some people are trading on human weakness so that they can live in luxury. We need to pray against this sort of evil. Are you prepared for the prayer battle which will come if

you feel called to pray in this area?

Drug users need love
Often drug users are rejected by society, and it's sometimes easy to see why. But God doesn't treat us in this way. We need to offer love and understanding wherever there is a need for it, however costly it may seem to us. This is easy to write, but hard to do. Are you willing to act in this way, if the need arises?

God can free people
Read this verse about Jesus:

"The Son of Man did not come to be served; he came to serve, and to give his life to redeem many people" (Mark 10:45).

By his death Jesus has set people free from the power of Satan. So he is able to free anyone – thief, murderer, drug addict, adulterer – from a lifestyle that is wrong. Jesus can set drug addicts free – through the work of drug rehabilitation centres or directly by the power of his Holy Spirit.

Jesus said that he had come to "proclaim liberty to the captives" (Luke 4:18). Do you believe that God can set the prisoners free? Or are you tempted to think that this is a problem which is beyond his control?

Have we failed?

Jesus has made us right with God (see John 1:12). Jesus didn't come to give us a bad deal: he came to give us real life – "life in all its fullness" (John 10:10). Like so many in our society, drug users have failed to hear this message. Have we, as individuals and as churches, failed to so live and speak about Jesus, that people have turned to drugs for that which we know Christ can give? Are you prepared to accept some of the blame, and begin to prepare yourself to share your faith? (See the last twenty pages of this book.)

HELP

If you've got involved in drugs — stop now, while you can. There's help around. Services available will be advertised in your local library. Your local Citizens Advice Bureau (find the number in the phone book) will be able to help you get in touch with those who can help.

Help and information for drug takers and those who want to help them can be got from:

- NAYPCAS (National Association of Young People's Counselling and Advisory Services), 17–23 Albion Street, Leicester LE1 6GD.
- SCODA (Standing Conference on Drug Abuse), 1–4 Hatton Place, Hatton Gardens, London EC1N 8ND. (You can just ring the operator and ask for Freephone Drug Problems, and you will get a recorded message giving you a contact in your area.)
- Narcotics Anonymous, PO Box 417, London SW10 0RS. Phone 01 351 6794.
- National Campaign Against Solvent Abuse, 309–13 Bon Marche Centre, 444 Brixton Road, London SW9. Phone 01 733 7330.
- Turning Point, CAP House, 9–12 Long Lane, London EC1A 9HA. Phone 01 606 3947.
- North Eastern Council on Addictions, 1 Mosely Street, Newcastle upon Tyne NE1 1YE.

AIDS

AIDS

Facts

AIDS is caused by a virus that can stop the body's normal defences against disease working. It kills because someone with the virus becomes open to all sorts of infections and diseases which their body can't resist.

Doesn't look too bad does it – especially when we read about thousands dying from famine, or caught up in a natural disaster? But the problem is that AIDS is fatal – and it's spreading. By the end of 1986, 300 people in Britain had died of AIDS in the five years since the first case was seen (1981). That may not seem much compared with 1100 deaths from alcohol-related car deaths each year. But the number of AIDS cases is doubling every 18 months, and at least 30,000 people are thought to be carrying the virus. If the present trends continue there could be about 5 million cases worldwide by the end of the century. This is what makes it so frightening.

And the real worry? There is no cure for AIDS, and there is no vaccine to safeguard people. AIDS is a death sentence, and in a society that has little idea of how to face death this makes AIDS one of the most feared diseases of all.

Think about it

Morality
AIDS shows up a basic problem in our society. Permissiveness has been the key word for so long that the idea of being a virgin until marriage and then being committed to that one partner for life has been pushed into the background. God clearly taught that a man and a woman are to be together sexually only in marriage – that's the 'one flesh' teaching touched on earlier (page 54). AIDS can be sexually transmitted and will spread through the community if people have sex with lots of different partners. The Government campaign in the face of AIDS was based on the slogan: 'Play safe, use a condom.' God's campaign is older and simpler – sex is for marriage. Drug users also risk infection if they share hypodermic needles, since the virus can be transferred from one person to another in a tiny drop of blood on a needle. Remember, though, that not all AIDS sufferers get AIDS through sex or drug abuse. Babies whose mothers have AIDS can have AIDS too.

Mortality
AIDS also shows up current attitudes to death. People don't like talking or thinking about death. Most dying is done in hospital, out of sight of most people. Few people have seen a dead body, and rumours and taboos about the dead are common. AIDS is forcing us to recognise our mortality. Death is something that Christians don't have to fear – and the Bible has a lot to say about coping with death. Have we been saying it loudly and clearly? When people have to face death, we should be there to help them. Are you

afraid of your own death? When others speak of death, do you make your Christian position clear? Look at the pages on death – 72–73.

God's judgment?
Is the outbreak of AIDS the judgment of God on people who have rejected his laws? Perhaps we should turn this idea around and put it like this – when men and women step outside of God's will and purpose things are bound to go wrong. (God doesn't want it this way – look at John 3:16–18 to see how Jesus came to put things right.) But that doesn't mean that if people suffer, they suffer *because* they are sinful. And remember: if God judged everyone who rejected his laws, we'd all be in big trouble sooner or later! How do you feel about this?

Compassion
Christians should be more concerned with being compassionate, and let God deal with judgment. We are here to help – to offer forgiveness and a new start, hope for the hopeless, and a strength in the face of death which nothing else can give. The moment we adopt any other position, we have to be very careful. We are not saying that there isn't sin and judgment involved, because there obviously is. But we are saying, 'God is loving, and is just waiting to put his arms around you.' How do you feel about this?

LOOK INTO THE BIBLE
Read this verse:

As he (Jesus) saw the crowds, his heart was filled with pity for them, because they were worried and helpless, like sheep without a shepherd (Matthew 9:36).

Ask God to give you compassion for those who have AIDS.

ACTION
If you're worried about AIDS there are a variety of things you can do.
● If you would like to talk to a trained advisor, call 0800 567 123. If you would like to order a free booklet, call 0800 555 777. (Both these 24 hour services are free and confidential.)
● You could contact the Genito-urinary Diseases (GU) Clinic. You'll find the number under 'Venereal Disease' in your local telephone directory.

Alcohol abuse

We all know the dangers of illegal drugs, but drinking, like smoking, can be as dangerous as illegal drugs and result in sorrow, tragedy and death.

Facts

- In Britain we spend more on alcohol (£35 million *a day* in 1989) than we do on clothes.
- Teenagers in Britain spend £227 million a year on alcohol. Alcohol is the main contributor to the deaths of young people – at least 1000 young people die from alcohol abuse each year. 80% of teenage drinkers have suffered some adverse consequences from drinking. One in fourteen fifth year boys regularly drink more than the safe limit for adult men.
- More than £200 million is spent each year on advertising alcohol.

- The government receives £7000 million a year from alcohol tax.

The hidden cost

Alcohol abuse costs Britain more than £2000 million each year in terms of lost days at work, damage to health, accidents and crime.
- 1 in 4 emergency admissions to hospital are attributed to alcohol abuse.
- 8–14 million days a year are lost at work because of heavy drinking.
- Alcohol is involved in a third of all accidents in the home, 19% of drownings, 52% of deaths from fires.

- Over 1100 people (the size of an average comprehensive school) die each year in road accidents caused by drunk drivers. Alcohol is a factor in nearly half of road accidents involving young people.
- 50% of all crime is linked with alcohol abuse, and drinking is a contributory factor in about half of all murders.

These statistics take no account of all the foolishness associated with alcohol abuse – the arguments, fights, insults, domestic violence and unpleasantness.

Think about it

1 Drunkenness is wrong

Read these verses:

Surely you know that you are God's temple and that God's Spirit lives in you! So if anyone destroys God's temple, God will destroy him. For God's temple is holy, and you yourselves are his temple (1 Corinthians 3:16–17).

This is not the first time that we have looked at these verses because they give us a clear reason as to why abuse (of any sort) is wrong. Alcohol abuse damages us – and we are very precious to God. It may seem funny to drink too much, but God doesn't find it very funny when we abuse our bodies in this way.

Do you think alcohol abuse is wrong? How do you stand by this belief when you're in a group who are settling down to drink too much.

2 God's in charge
Read this verse:

"Worship no god but me" (Exodus 20:3).

When a man or a woman is a slave to alcohol, he or she has denied the basic principle of the Christian faith – there is one God and we are to worship him, not the god of the bottle. So alcohol abuse is a spiritual problem – it offends God. Have you ever offended God in this way? Ask for his forgiveness now, and ask him to show you a better way.

3 Excess leads to excess
Read this verse:

Drinking too much makes you loud and foolish. It's stupid to get drunk (Proverbs 20:1).

When a man or woman drinks to excess, many other excesses follow – bad language and violence, dangerous foolishness, reckless driving, perhaps unwanted pregnancy, even rape and murder. We become loud and foolish and look ridiculous. Once we lose control of ourselves we give the evil one maximum room to damage us and others.
● Have you ever done something – because you'd been drinking – that you now regret? Repent of it right now (see 'Forgiveness – God's way', page 40).

4 Stay cool!
People drink to excess for so many reasons. What starts as a small drink to keep up with others, to stay in with the gang, to have a bit of 'fun', or to lose our inhibitions, becomes a crutch that we cannot live without. Once we're addicted, escaping is hard. Christians know that all these things – freedom from tension, easing of pressure, a sense of belonging – are provided through God's love.

▲ *Non-alcoholic drinks can look good – and taste great!*

We have a responsibility to live this fact out, so that more and more people can come to him rather than to drink.

What can I do?

There are a number of things you can do. As you do them, be gracious and determined.
1 Your own attitude to drink. Make sure you know what you think about alcohol – and make some firm decisions *before* you go to that party! (It's too late when you're there.) Know exactly how much you want to drink, especially in a group. Stick to soft drinks to be on the safe side. What do you think about non-alcoholic beers and wines?
2 If you know anyone with a drink problem, be compassionate and loving. Pray and look for chances to help if possible. (Look in the phone book under 'Alcohol' for agencies who can help you know what to do.)
3 Challenge attitudes. How about adopting these?
● Getting drunk is not an adult thing to do – it's something only fools do.

● Drinking and driving is very dangerous. Discourage it in every way.
● Under age drinking is not clever – it's stupid, against the law, and dishonouring to God.

Advertising that glamourises drink leads weak people into trouble. Should it be allowed? Tell your MP if you think things need changing.

HELP
If you have got a problem with alcohol, then the most adult thing you can do is to recognise it and get help. Only a fool refuses to ask for help. Alcoholics Anonymous (Al Anon) has a branch near you, and it will be listed in the phone book and advertised in the library. Their centre is: Alcoholics Anonymous GB PO Box 1, Stonebow House, Stonebow, York YO1 2NJ but they can be contacted by phone on 01 352 3001.
Al Ateen (an Al Anon type group for teenagers who've a relative with a drink problem) are at 61 Great Dover Street, London SE1 4YF. Phone 01 403 0888.

Abortion

Facts

In 1966 it was estimated that about 100,000 illegal abortions were performed annually in Britain. In an attempt to stop this illegal practice, and so to make abortion safer, the government of the day introduced the 1967 Abortion Act, which allowed legal termination of pregnancy if:
1 the life of the mother is at greater risk by continuing with the pregnancy than by terminating it.
2 the physical or mental health of the mother is more likely to be injured by continuing with the pregnancy than by terminating it.
3 the physical or mental health of any existing children are more likely to be injured by continuing with the pregnancy than by terminating it.
4 there is a substantial chance that the baby may suffer from such physical or mental abnormalities as to be seriously handicapped.

A doctor may perform an abortion on a woman over 16 subject to these conditions. Anyone under the age of 16 needs the permission of one parent/guardian.

Abortions can be performed in various ways. Early on in the pregnancy a tube may be inserted into the womb through the vagina and the contents of the womb sucked out. Alternatively the neck of the womb may be opened slightly and the contents scraped out. For more advanced pregnancies a drip (containing a special fluid) is put into the arm and this fluid causes the womb to expel the foetus. Late abortions may also be performed surgically.

Think about it

1 Ending life – God's responsibility

Job, one of the people written about in the Old Testament, said this after a great disaster had destroyed his family:

"The LORD gave, and now he has taken away. May his name be praised" (Job 1:21).

These words sum up the Christian position – only God gives life and only God can take it away. If this applies to you and me, then it applies to unborn babies too. These are hard words, but there's no way around this clear biblical position.

2 Is abortion ever okay?

If the life of a mother is put at risk by continuing with a pregnancy then almost everyone would agree that abortion could be permitted. This sort of case is very rare indeed and most abortions are carried out for other reasons.

3 Handicapped babies?

Looking after a handicapped baby can be very hard on the parents, and the baby will grow into a handicapped adult who may need a lot of care. But it's not all hard slog: being with handicapped people is almost always rewarding and is often great fun – it's not all doom and gloom. Anyway – the Bible does not give us permission to destroy a foetus because the baby may be handicapped – handicapped people have the same rights as you and me.

4 Abortion is OK because. . . . .

Many reasons are given to justify the practice of abortion. Here are some of them – what do you feel about them?

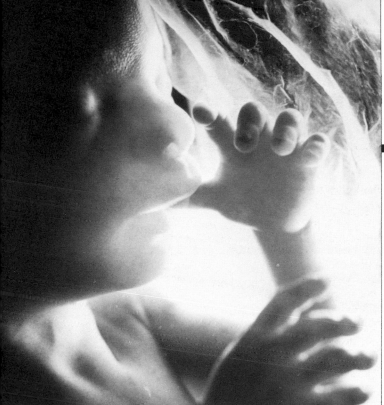

LINK: Boy meets girl . . . (page 32)

◀ *This baby is just 18 weeks old.*

Avoid a situation in which you or your partner may be offered an abortion – think through what you think about sex. See 'Sex', page 54.

2 Say, 'No'

If your boyfriend or family are pressuring you to have an abortion, resist them – and think through what you are doing. There are people who can help advise you, but don't jump into having an abortion before having time to think and pray. Here are some sources of help.

● Family doctors and hospitals may be able to put you in touch with people who can talk things through with you.

● Many pro-life groups advertise in public places, giving you a number to call. (Look in the library.)

● Write to LIFE, 118–120 Warwick Street, Leamington Spa, Warwickshire CV32 4QY (0926 21587) or CARE, 53 Romney Street, London SW1P 3RF (01 233 0455).

3 Be compassionate

Most of us know women who have had abortions. These women need our love and concern. Even if what they have done is wrong in God's eyes, our first reaction must be a loving and caring one. Is this true for you?

If you have had an abortion and this article has made you feel that you have hurt God, then be comforted – God is a forgiving and healing God, not a hard and unloving person. Turn to the pages on forgiveness (page 40) and find someone you can talk to – your minister (if you have one) or a friend at school. Don't feel condemned – God loves and forgives his children.

● 'It's my body.'

Jesus said, "I have been given all authority in heaven and on earth" (Matthew 28:18).

One of the expressions often used to justify abortion is this: 'A woman has the right to say what happens in her body.' The Bible, however, says something different. All rights belong to Jesus, not to us. He controls the world and everything in it. He alone has the right to say what should happen.

● 'I couldn't cope.' This is a common reason given for wanting an abortion. You and I can help by supporting such people so that abortion isn't the only way out. (CARE do this: write to them at the address at the end of this unit.)

● 'I didn't want it.' If the pregnancy is inconvenient or a moral embarrassment, an abortion may seem a means of removing the problem. But we need to challenge those who see a new life as less important than an inconvenience.

● 'It's better than having unwanted children.' Some people argue that abortion is better than lots of unwanted and possibly ill-treated children. This has to be put into a Biblical framework. What's being said is that to end the life of an unborn baby is better than inconvenience, a lack of love or a poor quality lifestyle. It's also not true – lots of unwanted children have been born since the Abortion Act, and tragically many are still ill-treated.

5 The man's responsibility

Only women can have abortions, but they didn't conceive the babies on their own. The rise in abortions is a challenge to the low morality of men in conceiving these babies, and the lack of spiritual understanding that men show in allowing their children to be aborted, rather than caring for them as is their responsibility.

Action!

1 Be pure

'Prevention is better than cure.'

Suffering +

Five years ago we had a baby called Philip. Sadly he was born very early, and in spite of all that the doctors could do he only lived for three hours. My wife and I found this a really tough experience at the time. In the years that have followed we've asked God again and again, 'Why did you let this happen to us? We believe in you, we really prayed hard, and so did many of our friends. Why didn't you answer us?'

● Has anything happened in your life which has made you ask the same question? Anyone really involved in the issues we've been looking at over the last few pages must have asked this question.

LINK: Death (page 72)

After many years of struggling, I still don't know why Philip died, or why God let it happen. If there were an easy answer I would have found it by now. But as I've tried to understand, I've been encouraged by the experience of Mary, the mother of Jesus. After her baby was born she went to the Temple to give thanks to God and, while she was there, she met a man called Simeon. He prayed for Mary and Jesus but his prayer had a very strange end:

"This child is chosen by God for the destruction and the salvation of many in Israel. He will be a sign from God which many people will speak against and so reveal their secret thoughts. And sorrow, like a sharp sword, will break your own heart" (Luke 2:34–35).

● If you had been Mary, how would you have felt about Simeon's words – "and sorrow like a sharp sword will break your own heart"? Yet that's exactly what happened to Mary. For many years later she was to watch the execution of her son.

Standing close to Jesus' cross were his mother, his mother's

70   ISSUES

sister, Mary the wife of Clopas, and Mary Magdalene. Jesus saw his mother and the disciple he loved standing there; so he said to his mother, "He is your son." Then he said to the disciple, "She is your mother." From that time the disciple took her to live in his home (John 19:25–27).

Not only did Mary see her son publicly humiliated and killed, she then had to leave her home and get used to living somewhere else. Remember that at the time she probably knew nothing of the coming resurrection of Jesus. Quite a sharp sword, wasn't it?

But Mary's experience can encourage us if we remember that although 'sharp swords' can't be avoided, they are not accidents which happen without God knowing about them. If we trust him, he is able to help us through and bring good out of every experience, however painful it may be for us at the time.
● Have you the courage and faith to call on God to help you through the bad times, bringing good from pain? You'll need courage to pray like this. (See Romans 8:28.)

Here are some encouragements for you, as you face the question of suffering.

1 The cross and me
At the centre of our faith stands a risen Christ and a wooden cross. If we want to share the joy of the risen Christ we must also be prepared to share the pain of the cross. Through the death of Philip, our little son, with all its pain and sorrow, we have grown much closer to Jesus. Somehow we understand more now the cost of the cross to him. We also

understand these words: "If anyone wants to come with me, he must forget self, carry his cross, and follow me" (Mark 8:34).
● Read the story of the death of Jesus in Mark 15. Ask God for a deeper understanding of the suffering of Jesus.

2 Our God reigns
Hold onto this truth, however painful the hard times are for you. No matter how black things may seem, Jesus really is Lord.
● Read Philippians 2:10–11 now. Ask God to show you something of his victory over all things.

3 God loves us
God loves us with a love that cannot be broken. He wants the very best for us, and he's too big to make mistakes, however bad things may seem. Sometimes it's hard to see where the love is, and in these times we must trust the promises of the Bible until the better times come.
● Read 1 John 4:10. Then ask God to let you feel his love more today.

4 It's only temporary
Our life on earth seems so important to us, especially when we're young. There's so much we want to do, and there seem to be years ahead for achieving our aims. Yet a lifetime can seem a long time if things get really tough. However, life on earth is short compared with eternity, and our sufferings won't seem much when seen against that background. Read Romans 8:18–25.
● Ask God to help you see things from his eternal point of view.

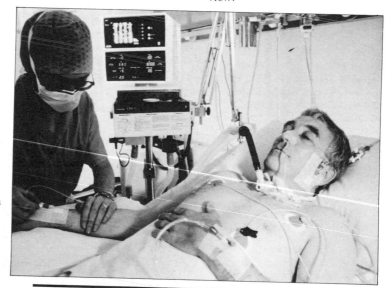

LOOK INTO THE BIBLE
When things are tough read Psalm 23 and Psalm 91.

DEATH

LINK: What do I believe about Jesus? (page 18)

There have been about 75 million deaths in England and Wales since official registration began in 1837. By estimating that the world was populated by human beings in 40,000 BC, a meeting of the British Association for the Advancement of Science concluded that up to 1980 there had been 60,000 million deaths in the world. The one figure which they don't mention, but which we all know about, is that from the beginning of time until now the death rate has remained at a steady 100%.

Death is going to affect every reader of this page, yet we spend very little time thinking about death. Why is this?

• Because we're young, and death is something that we think only happens to adults – especially old adults.

• Because it's something to be afraid of, and one way of coping with fear is to pretend that what we fear isn't there, that it will go away, or that it won't come to us.

• Because our society has put death out of sight – people die in hospitals, where no one sees them. It isn't part of our daily experience, so we forget about it.

But let's be honest for a minute. We all know that we will die – no one reading this will be alive in the year 2100. So:

• have you ever thought about your own death?

• have you ever discussed this matter with your friends?

• are you frightened or uncertain about death, and what will follow afterwards?

• do you have sad feelings inside of you because of the death of a family member or friend?

DEATHS

GOUGH: Campbell, husband and father. On Friday 13 October, aged 82. Funeral at Golder's Green Crematorium, Tuesday 24 October, 2.30pm.

MORGAN: On 17 October 1989, as a result of a car accident, Alex. Funeral 2.30pm, Tuesday, St Faiths, Worcester. No flowers, donations to St Faiths. Memorial Service, to be announced later.

Mahon: Andrew, of King's Lynn, 11 October.

Pettigrew: Elaine, 12 October.

Totteridge: Rebecca in Guildford, 17 October.

Williams: Thomas, of Colchester, 15 October.

Yardley: Erica Rose, of Tunbridge Wells, 13 October.

There is a Christian answer to death.

Do not be afraid

Read these verses:

Jesus himself became like them and shared their human nature. He did this so that through his death he might destroy the Devil, who has the power over death, and in this way set free those who were slaves all their lives because of their fear of death (Hebrews 2:14–15).

Christians do not need to be afraid of death, because Jesus has already dealt with it.

Jesus has the power

Read these words:

"Don't be alarmed. I know you are looking for Jesus of Nazareth, who was crucified. He is not here – he has been raised! Look, here is the place where they put him" (Mark 16:6).

These words were spoken to the women who went to anoint the body of Jesus on the first Easter day. When they looked in the burial cave they didn't see a body, only a man dressed in white, who told them about the resurrection of Jesus. Throughout his life, Jesus had shown that he had the power to raise the dead – he raised Lazarus, a widow's son, a little girl – now that same power had been used to raise him.

We share Jesus' victory

Read these words: "I am telling you the truth: he who believes has eternal life" (John 6:47). Jesus doesn't keep his victory over death to himself. If we believe in him, we will share it as well. That's his promise to us.

3 *Be confident.* Maybe some of your friends are afraid of death – then you have a very special message for them, the message of Christ's victory. Why not share this page with them, your own feelings about death, and your faith in Jesus (see the last twenty pages of this book). You never know how much they may be longing to talk about this subject and to hear about the Christian faith.

Something to learn:
'Christ has died,
Christ is risen,
Christ will come again.'
Something to read: 1 Corinthians 15:50–58.

What can I do now?

1 *Be certain.* No matter how bad things seem around you, you do not need to be afraid of death. You may be nervous about the process of dying – most of us are – but there is no need to fear death itself. Spend a few moments reading Hebrews 2:14–15 and ask Jesus to take away from you any fear of death that you might have.

2 *Be comforted.* Perhaps you have some sad feelings inside you because of the death of someone you love. Jesus understands these feelings – just as he understood the feelings of Martha and Mary in the story of Lazarus (John 11) and of his own mother at his death (John 19:25–27). Spend a few moments sharing how you feel with Jesus and, if you can, share them with a Christian friend. When our baby son died we found that sharing our sorrow was a great help.

These words (from Philippians 1:21) were written on the coffin lid of William Grimshaw, a Christian minister who died in the 17th century: 'For me to live is Christ, to die is gain.' These words are written on the tombstone of Martin Luther King, a famous Christian of this century: 'Free at last! Free at last! Thank God I'm free at last.'

Miracles

I got a letter recently from a reader of JAM magazine. He said: 'My friends say they believe in God, but can't understand how he works miracles. What can I say to them?'

Understand the problem

Many people wonder about miracles, for a mixture of reasons.

• They've never seen one, so they don't believe they can happen.

• Miracles seem 'unscientific', and therefore some people say they cannot happen.

• There are many phoney miracles around, and people can't tell the false ones from the true ones – so they disbelieve them all.

Miracles are even a problem (of a different sort) to believers. They seem never to happen when we want them, and they *do* happen when we don't expect them. When we're trying to get our thinking right about miracles it's important to remember that God, unlike us, has no problem with them. As Jesus said: "What is impossible for man is possible for God" (Luke 18:27). And he lived by this statement – he healed the sick, controlled nature, set people free from demons, and raised the dead.

Christians believe miracles are possible, because we believe that Jesus always tells the truth. If he says nothing is impossible, then that's the truth as far as we are concerned. It's much more important for us, however, to know *why* God does miracles, rather than *how* he does them.

▲ *True miracles point to God.*

Then we'll be able to answer our friends' doubts and, at the same time, tell the true miracles from the false ones.

Why does God do miracles?

1 Not for show
Again and again, Jesus refused to do miracles if people just wanted to see something sensational (see Mark 8:12.) In many cases he did miracles privately, and encouraged those healed to go home quietly rather than to go rushing around causing a big stir.

2 Out of love
Many of the miracles which Jesus did came about because he was concerned for those who were ill, or suffering. Jesus really did have a heart full of love and compassion and, through his miracles, he was letting us see and understand something of that love. (See Luke 7:11–17.)

3 A challenge to believe
Miracles don't only benefit those who are healed. They also challenge the faith of those who witnessed the miracles. After Jesus had raised Lazarus from the dead, for example, some of

those who saw it believed in Jesus, but others refused to believe in him (see John 11:45–57). True miracles are very evangelistic – they challenge people to decide where they stand, and to accept or reject Jesus.

Miracles – and us

What sort of attitude should we have to miracles today?

1 Expect them

People often refuse to believe in miracles because they can't be proved scientifically. But we must not get trapped into believing that unless science can explain it, it can't happen. God is bigger than any scientific explanation, and we must always be prepared for him to do unexpected and unusual things.
● Do you expect God to be doing wonderful things?

2 Let them increase our faith

God doesn't do miracles on demand or just for fun. Any modern miracle must increase faith and bring glory to God. If it doesn't do this then we must look at it with some doubt. But if we see or read of miracles that are genuine then we should let our own faith be strengthened.
● Is your faith being strengthened by what God is doing today?

3 They must bring glory to God

Many people claim to be able to perform miracles, or to have experienced them. When considering these experiences remember that God is a God of the impossible, but not the ridiculous. Statues that apparently move or weep tears bring much attention on TV but do little to bring glory to God.
● See if the miracles you see or read about fit the 'why' reasons above. Then you won't be fooled, or be made to look stupid.

4 Let them challenge

Miracles are meant to challenge those who don't believe in Jesus. If people refuse to believe that Jesus can raise the dead, they haven't really fully understood who he is. Explain the facts of Jesus and challenge them to accept him for themselves. Remember, the greatest miracle of all is that Jesus died for you, and that now you belong to him. We long that our friends will know this miracle as well, don't we?

5 God rules

Our God can do anything. He's the King of kings and Lord of lords. See Philippians 2:9–11. All authority and power has been given to him. If he wants to do a miracle in your life, then be ready and willing for him to do it. But if he doesn't, still love and praise him. If he does miracles in other people's lives then apply the biblical tests and, if all seems right, be glad for them and thank God.

CHECK IT OUT

To 'test' a miracle ask –
● does God get the glory, or does the one who performed the miracle get it?
● does the performer of the miracle refuse any credit, glory or payment?
● does it show the love and concern of God?
● does it challenge faith?
● does it in any way make God look ridiculous?

◀ *Jesus did a lot with five loaves and two fish.*

Other faiths

LINK: What do I believe about Jesus? (page 18)

There was a time when to meet with people of other faiths we would have had to go to other lands, but that's no longer true. It's quite common now in some schools to have assemblies for Christians on some days and for Muslims on another. Many towns now have a mosque, or at least a place where Muslims worship. Britain is now multicultural: and some of the many cultures represented involve following other faiths. This can all be very confusing for Christians. What do these other religions teach? Are they right or wrong? What should my attitude be?

The best way to get an answer to these questions is to study the documents and teachings of other religions. But this can be very time consuming and confusing! So here are some basic 'rules' – some guidelines which I've found useful as I have worked with and witnessed to people of other faiths.

1 No compromise

The Bible teaches us quite clearly that there is only *one way* to get right with God, and that is through Jesus. Read and learn this verse:

"I am the way, the truth, and the life; no one goes to the Father except by me" (John 14:6).

When we get involved with people of other faiths, this should be our position.

2 Awareness of God

Read this verse:

"For everyone who asks will receive, and anyone who seeks will find, and the door will be opened to him who knocks" (Matthew 7:8).

People who believe in another god have an awareness that human beings are spiritual beings, with a need to get their lives right with God. They have some awareness of spiritual things. Millions of people worshipping in other faiths know that they have a need to worship. This gives us a starting point, from which we can share God's love.

3 Love and humility

We must approach people of other faiths in the right way, in the same way that Christ approached us – loving us and serving us (see 1 John 4:10 and Philippians 2:5–11). This approach will allow us to make friends, not enemies – and that's the place to start. If we are loving and caring then we are showing the love of God.

4 Care enough to share

If we truly love people of other faiths then we're going to want to talk to them about Jesus. If we don't, then we don't truly love them. We need to be sensitive and caring, but we've no need to be afraid of other faiths – why should we be? But we are often afraid, either because we are ignorant of their ways and customs or because we don't want to feel foolish. But you will find that people of other faiths will often be more open to talk about Jesus than people who have no faith at all. But we're also afraid because we don't know much about their faith, and so we feel inhibited in speaking about ours. So it's best to stick to what you do know.

● How you became a Christian and what this means for you.

● The simple facts of Jesus' life, death and resurrection.

● The need to respond to him.

If we do this because we love and care for other people then we are giving the Holy Spirit the best possible material to work on. It's also worth remembering that people of other faiths might be as ignorant of what we believe as we are about what they believe.

IN THE PICTURE
It does help a lot if we are able to understand a little about Islam (what Muslims believe), Hinduism and Sikhism. Why not ask your minister/youth group leader or look in your local library or Christian bookshop?

THIRD WORLD ISSUES

A while ago I was watching awful pictures on TV of floods which had hit Bangladesh. I felt so sad for all the people who were homeless, and wished that there was something I could do for them. Have you ever felt like this?

In the face of natural disasters on the other side of the world, people often feel helpless. But one of the things that excited me as a Christian is that there's lots I can do to help people in other countries. Our God is so big that he can do anything! So what can I do to help people in other lands?

1 Care!

God really cares about the poor and needy, and he wants us to do the same. Jesus told a story about the final judgment, including a conversation between himself and those who had cared for people in need. Read these words:

"The righteous will then answer him, 'When, Lord, did we ever see you hungry and feed you, or thirsty and give you a drink? When did we ever see you a stranger and welcome you in our homes, or naked and clothe you? When did we ever see you sick or in prison, and visit you?' The King [Jesus] will reply, 'I tell you, whenever you did this for one of the least important of these brothers of mine, you did it for me!'" (Matthew 25:37–40.)

But we will only share God's feelings for the poor if we spend time with God and ask him to change the way we feel. Have you got the courage to do this? Anything might happen if you pray a prayer like this: 'Father, I know that you care about the poor. I want to share that concern. I surrender myself to you right now. Help me to do what you want done.'

2 Value others

We are all precious to God – he says that even the hairs of our head are numbered. (See Luke 12:6–7.) But it's easy to think that people in the west have got everything to give and to teach to the third world, and this can so easily turn into a 'looking down' attitude. But we are all of equal value to God, and have much to give each other. We are in a partnership together, as we live in God's world. Is this your attitude?

3 Learn about others

If we're really concerned for other lands then it's essential that we learn about them, so that we can show our concern in practical and sensible ways. We can't learn about everywhere, so why not select one country and learn all you can about it? Then you'll know its needs and be able to pray and give in a right way. I have a number of countries on my prayer list – Cambodia and Nepal are two of them. I watch out for them on

ADDRESSES

TEAR Fund, 100 Church Road, Teddington, Middlesex TW11 8QE

Save the Children Fund, 17 Grove Lane, London SE5 8RD

Christian Aid, 35 Lower Marsh Street, London SE1

Oxfam, 274 Banbury Road, Oxford, OX2 7JF

Catholic Fund for Overseas Development, 2 Romero Close, Stockwell Road, London SW9 9TY

Methodist Relief and Development Fund, 1 Central Buildings, Westminster, London SW1H 9NH

the news, pray for people there, look for them in the papers, read books about them – and I've found that I really do feel a part of these lands. Why not join me? Your church, school CU or youth fellowship could 'adopt' a country, and get information from agencies like TEAR Fund or Christian Aid. The question is – do you care enough to make the effort?

4 Live a simple life

Why not live a more simple lifestyle, as a way of identifying with the people of the poorer lands? There are many ways of working this out in practice.
- Fast once a week, and give some money to help the poor.
- Spend less on clothes, and give the extra money away.
- Live simply, especially at Christmas. Don't get caught up in materialism.

There are many more ways of living simply, as a sign of caring for the poor of the world. The question is – do you have the courage and the will to do it?

5 Give

It isn't enough just to be concerned for the third world. We have to give so that needs are met. (Read 1 John 3:17–18.) There are many ways of giving.
- The poor sometimes need money just to stay alive – give to them through the aid agencies.
- The poor need more of our national wealth to develop economically – so that the world can be a fairer place. Write to your MP encouraging him or her to support development programmes.
- The poor need their situation to be known. Tell your friends or write to the local radio stations about situations in the world that you want publicised.
- The poor need friends. Try to help your friends and colleagues understand the needs of the poor.
- The poor need people – is God calling you to work for the poor of the third world?
- Most of all, refuse to give up your desire to serve the poor, and try to get others to be concerned for the poor.

And remember – God never gave up on us, and we shouldn't give up sharing with other people in the third world.

ADOPT A COUNTRY
Why not –
- choose a country which is poorer than yours.
- find out all you can about it.
- get others in your church or Christian group to care too – and to pray.
- do all you can to support hungry people in the country you have chosen.

DO SOMETHING
Why not –
- fast on one day each week.
- give money to relief and development work.
- give up something – as a sign that you want to stand alongside those who are poor.

SPIRITUAL GIFTS

LINK: The Holy Spirit (page 8)

We've already looked at the Holy Spirit and his place in the life of a Christian. One of the signs of his presence are the gifts he gives to us. ('Gifts' means the ability to do certain things – not a box wrapped in shining paper!) These gifts have become much more common in recent years and we need to know where we stand on them.

The facts

1 The gifts that the Holy Spirit has to give come from him. The Bible teaches us:

There are different kinds of spiritual gifts, but the same Spirit gives them (1 Corinthians 12:4).

They are real gifts – presents from him to us. We don't have to earn them, we don't deserve them, and there's no way we can buy them. (Simon Magus tried to do this, with disastrous results – see Acts 8:9–25.)

2 All Christians have some of the gifts – maybe more than we know. No one is left out – the Bible teaches:

The Spirit's presence is shown in some way in each person for the good of all (1 Corinthians 12:7).

We may not be clear what our gifts are, but we do have one (or some).

3 The gifts have a purpose. Gifts are to be enjoyed, but the gifts of the Holy Spirit have a purpose. The Bible says: 'The Spirit's presence is shown in some way in each person for the good of all.' The gifts God gives are meant to be used for the good of others. We may enjoy having them, and using them, but they're for the strengthening and growth of the church.

4 There are many gifts. Some of the gifts of the Holy Spirit are listed in the Bible, but it's important to realise that these are general headings. Just as the word 'tree' covers hundreds of varieties, so these titles of gifts cover hundreds of varieties. Romans 12:6–8 speaks about gifts of speaking God's message, serving, teaching, encouraging, sharing and more. Look them up for yourself. In 1 Corinthians 12:4–11 we can read about gifts of the power to heal, the power to work miracles, the power to speak in languages we've never learned (this is called 'speaking in tongues') – or to interpret them – and many others. And a couple of spiritual gifts – preaching and serving – are mentioned in 1 Peter 4:10–11.

One of the best ways to understand the Holy Spirit, how he works and what he gives, is to see him in action. The book called The Acts of the Apostles allows us to do just that. Why not read this book, a chapter a day, for the next month?

CHECK IT OUT
Read the lists of the gifts of the Spirit given in Romans 12 and 1 Corinthians 12. Talk them over with friends. Ask:
- what is each gift?
- how can it be divided up into its many varieties?

- how do we know if we have a particular gift – how would it show?

The gifts and me

1 Discover your gifts

In our house on Christmas morning there are presents under the tree. We adults sit back and have a cup of tea before we discover ours. Not so my son Stephen. He jumps straight in, shouting, 'Which one's for me!' He doesn't doubt that there is a present for him – it's just a question of which one. The same is true with the gifts of the Spirit. There's one – maybe more than one – just for you. So start asking the Holy Spirit to show you what he has given you. Pray and read the Bible; talk it over with Christian friends. Be excited – this is a great experience of the Christian life.

2 Don't be afraid

Some people are afraid of the Holy Spirit. They think that he will make them do things that they wouldn't want to do, or will make them look a fool. I was like this at first, and hesitated to ask him for the gifts he had given to me. But I soon discovered that the Holy Spirit isn't a harsh person – he's gentle and caring, and loves me and you deeply. The Bible teaches us that perfect love drives out all fear. Ask the Holy Spirit to help you love him more.

3 Don't be confused

There has been a lot of confusion about the gifts of the Spirit in our churches.

- Some people have refused to admit that he has gifts to give.
- Some people – because they are afraid – have tried to stop those who believe that he is at work today from saying so.
- Some people have problems with gifts like healing, prophecy and speaking in tongues. They can't imagine that God could work like this.
- Some people who have gifts have said foolish things, like, 'You can't be a Christian without speaking in tongues', for example, and have behaved in a foolish and arrogant way to those who didn't believe quite the same as they did.
- Some people have claimed to have spiritual gifts but live rotten lives. As a result of this, some Christians have hesitated to try and find their gifts.

In all of this there are some simple rules to guide us.
- *Loving and caring?* The Holy Spirit is loving and caring. If people claim gifts but are hard and arrogant, we have a right to question their claims.
- *Humble and joyful?* The Holy Spirit does give gifts. People who have them and who are walking humbly and closely with Jesus will be a joy to know. Their genuineness and honesty will shine through.
- *Past mistakes?* Mistakes of the past mustn't be allowed to stop us moving forward with the Spirit today. Don't write off spiritual gifts. Check it out – and stick to what the Bible says.

Sharing Jesus :

I recently had a letter from someone who wants to share her faith with her family but never seems to get the opportunity, or when it comes she never knows what to say. She writes: 'I feel such a failure. What can I do?'

As Christians, we all have the responsibility to share our faith with others. The Bible makes this quite clear:

Be ready at all times to answer anyone who asks you to explain the hope you have in you (1 Peter 3:15).

But for most of us, it never seems quite so easy as Peter makes it appear. Like the person who wrote to me, we never seem to get the right chance or, when we do, we say the wrong things. Most of us feel like this, so don't be discouraged if you do as well. It's quite possible however that many of our problems come because we start in the wrong place. Evangelism starts not with *us* but with God.

God cares!

We're often so keen to get on and do things that we forget that evangelism (sharing our faith) starts with God. As we spend time with God, so we will want to share our experience of him with others – but it all starts by spending time with him. This was Isaiah's experience. He had a great vision of God (see Isaiah 6) and when, at the end of the vision, God said, "Whom shall I send? Who will be our messenger?" Isaiah quickly replied: "I will go. Send me." He had spent time with God, and was willing to respond.

● If you want to share your faith with others, start off by spending more time with God in prayer

and worship. This is not time wasted, but is the right place to start. Evangelism starts with God, and continues in the power of the Holy Spirit.

The Holy Spirit

We can do nothing for God by ourselves. We need the Holy Spirit to give us the ability (see Acts 1:8) and to help others see their need for Jesus. (See John 16:5–15.)

● Have you been trying to go it alone? Ask the Holy Spirit to give you a deeper desire for others, the ability to speak about Jesus, and the desire in others to want to hear what you have to say. But that's not all – evangelism will challenge the way we live.

Lifestyle

'OK,' I hear you saying, 'I'll spend more time with God, call on the Holy Spirit, and then I'll get on with it.' But it doesn't work that way either! The way we live has got to reflect the God we are sharing. Otherwise we're living a lie, and those we want to win for Christ will soon see it. Read these stories:

—Living and Loving—

Two men went out visiting to speak to local people about Jesus. One person was very interested, and invited the men to return next week. When they came back he was not interested, and when the men asked why, replied, 'I saw one of you drunk at the pub on Saturday. If that's how Christians live, I want no part of it.'

Mary and Jim had a baby who died soon after he was born. They were very hurt by this but still continued to believe and trust in Jesus. A friend who was not a Christian, when he saw that they still believed in Jesus, said, 'I'm amazed at Mary and Jim. They've gone on believing, despite everything that has happened. That must be some powerful God they believe in.'

The lives we lead are key factors in opening or closing people to the message of Jesus.
● Let the Holy Spirit examine your life today. What needs repenting of, or changing? Are there things you do which you think are all right, but which might stop others believing?

If we're trying to live close to God, have asked for his help in sharing Jesus and are ready to start – where do we begin? The answer is in prayer: but that's such a big topic that you'll have to turn over the page and find what's written there. The last step in sharing Jesus might seem obvious, and it's making friends with people.

Friendships

On that same day two of Jesus' followers were going to a village named Emmaus, about eleven kilometres from Jerusalem, and they were talking to each other about all the things that had happened. As they talked and discussed, Jesus himself drew near and walked along with them; they saw him, but somehow did not recognize him (Luke 24:13–15).

Jesus was planning a real surprise for these two disciples, and it all began as he came alongside them and began to talk with them. This is one of the secrets of sharing – we need to get alongside people, to get to know them, and to make friends with them. Then these friendships open the way for sharing what we know about Jesus. Read this:

A university CU was planning a mission and the small group running it met with me to discuss preparations. When I asked them about their week they replied, 'On Monday it's planning committee. On Tuesday the prayer group, Wednesday the house fellowship, Thursday the fellowship and on Friday our Christian Union meeting.' So I asked, 'When are you going to build friendships, so that people can hear about Christ?'

When are you?

THE STORY SO FAR
1 Time with God
2 The power of the Holy Spirit
3 Prayer
4 Lifestyle
5 Friendships

Evangelism is a sequence of events — a chain with many links. We all have a part to play. Where do you fit in?

Sharing:
CARING & PRAYING

I was once speaking at a week-long evangelistic outreach in a church. Despite all our efforts very few people were giving their lives to Jesus. So I asked for more prayer and that night, as I stood up to preach, the prayer group was meeting in a room just behind me. They were praying so hard that, as I spoke, I could hear them praying even through the wall! What's more, so could the front six rows of people! But God heard them, and not only were there many people who came to Jesus that night, but many more followed throughout the rest of the week.

Prayer changes things. It is a very powerful weapon for us to use in the job of sharing Jesus with other people. As we pray for others we are working with God to make our friends more open to him.

Can you pray for others – pray that they will come to know Jesus? If you can, and you're willing to go on praying and praying until they do respond, then you're in the front line of evangelism. I learnt many years ago that it's prayer that changes lives. How can we pray in such a way that people do respond to Jesus?

1 Pray, and believe it!

God has said, "Call to me, and I will answer you; I will tell you wonderful and marvellous things that you know nothing about" (Jeremiah 33:3). Jesus said, "I will do whatever you ask for in my name, so that the Father's glory will be shown through the Son" (John 14:13). 'For we do not know how we ought to pray; the Spirit himself pleads with God for us in groans that words cannot express' (Romans 8:26).

2 Prayer triplets

Two men can resist an attack that would defeat one man alone. A rope made of three cords is hard to break (Ecclesiastes 4:12).

Prayer triplets have become very common these days. They work like this.

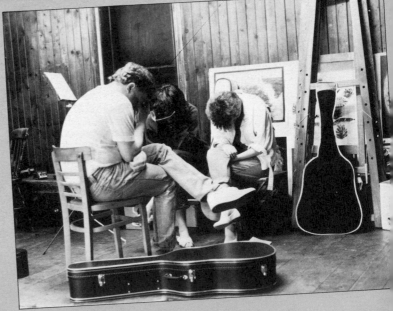

These verses give us enough encouragement to get praying in the name of Jesus, believing that those we ask for will, in the end, come to know Jesus. Don't worry about asking for the wrong things or people – it's always right to pray that people will come to know Jesus.

• Make a list of three people that you would like to see come to know Jesus.
• Find two other people who have also made lists.
• Agree to meet at least once a fortnight to pray for all nine people on your lists.

This is such an easy way to pray for others. Not only is much prayer prayed, but we encourage each other.

3 'Andrew' prayer

At once he (Andrew) found his brother Simon and told him, "We have found the Messiah." (This word means "Christ.") Then he took Simon to Jesus (John 1:41).

Here is another good method of prayer, especially if you are wanting people to come to an evangelistic meeting of some kind.
1 Select seven people that you would like to see come to the meetings.
2 Give each person a day of the week.
3 Pray for each person on their particular day. It's good to make this prayer specific.
● Pray that you will have a chance to speak to them, and to build your friendship with them.
● Pray that you will have a chance to invite them to a meeting – but that if you don't, someone else will.
● Pray that they will want to come.

With this prayer behind us, you'll be amazed when the people on your 'Andrew' list agree to come with you to a meeting.

4 Concentrated prayer

So Peter was kept in jail, but the people of the church were praying earnestly to God for him (Acts 12:5).

There are some occasions when special times of prayer for evangelism should be held. Could your church, fellowship or CU arrange a
● lunchtime prayer meeting,
● evening of prayer,
● day of prayer,
● half night of prayer,
● day of prayer and fasting?

These determined times of prayer can bring great results – see the rest of the story of Peter in Acts 12.

THE STORY SO FAR
1 Time with God
2 The power of the Holy Spirit
3 Prayer
4 Lifestyle
5 Friendships

Where do you fit in? Where do some of your close friends fit in? Can you help them find their place? Why not run a Saturday 'Sharing Course' – a day of training for Christians based on the material in this section?

Sharing :

When we think about sharing Jesus with our friends, it's easy to make the mistake of thinking that we've got to share everything all at once. Some people can do this, but for most of us, sharing is a gradual process – first prayer, then a growing friendship, and then. . . . . The most natural thing to share with others is the story of how we came to know Jesus for ourselves. We can be quite confident in this because:

- it's the truth.
- it comes naturally.
- it's a story, and most people like stories, and will listen.

(That's partly why Jesus told so many parables.)

But we often fail to take the opportunity to tell our story, because we haven't got it sorted out into some order. It's worth doing that, and here's one way of doing it.

My story

1 Write down the story of how you came to know Jesus. It doesn't have to be neat – short phrases and words will do. Make sure you include:
- how you started to think about God.
- how you came to know Jesus.
- what difference knowing him has made to your life.
- what difference he makes today, with one example from the last two weeks.

This last bit is the part of your story which really packs a punch, and it's the bit that's often left out. It's what God has done for you *today* that really affects people. It may be a big thing – calmed exam nerves, a successful operation, protection from a disaster – or a small thing – someone saying something encouraging, finding something you had lost, a sense of being loved by God. It's important that you are able to say that you asked God for these things, and that you feel he has answered.

2 Leave that list in a safe place for a day or two. This gives the Holy Spirit a chance to bring to your mind anything that you may have left out.

3 Come back to your list and read it through. Is there anything you want to change? Then do it.

4 Now write it out longhand, and leave it for a few days.

5 When you come back to it, read it through and ask:
- how long did it take to read?
- how could I use it with my friends – would they get bored?
- are there one or two good illustrations I should add?

6 Find a Christian friend and read it to him or her. Ask him what he thought and make any

My Story

changes that you both think will improve it.

7 Practise saying it a few times, until you can say it without notes.

Getting stuck with this job? Then remember that the story of how you came to know Jesus is *powerful*. It's true, and it sets people thinking. (Remember when you're writing your story that there are two ways of coming to know Jesus. One is the 'before and after' experience. People in this group remember clearly the time when they did not know Jesus. The other group is the 'always' group. These people cannot remember a time when they didn't know Jesus. When writing their story the 'always' group merely leave out the 'before' section. We concentrate on what it means to know God personally, and the difference this has made to our lives.)

Getting started

How do we move from having this story in our minds, to sharing it? This often worries people, but it shouldn't. All we need is a simple lead-in which will help us move on to talking about Jesus. We're not trying to do the Holy Spirit's job, or force ourselves on others. We're just trying to make ourselves more useful to the Spirit, when he calls on us to share. Here are two examples.

You start

'What do you do in your spare time. . . . .'
   'I usually go out on a Friday night. I play footie on Saturday. What do you do?'
'Normally on a Friday I go to our church youth club.'
'CHURCH!'
'Yes, going to church may seem crazy – but it's not. Can I tell you why . . .?' Then you're into your story.

They start

'Where did you go this weekend?'
   'Church.'
   'CHURCH!!!'
   'Yes . . . it's really great. Would you like to know why I go?' Then you're off!

Getting finished

But what do we do when we've told our story? No problem – either change the subject, ask them if they've any questions, or offer them a booklet: 'This will tell you all about it, Jim.'

Don't drop them!

● Keep praying.
● Look for opportunities to invite them somewhere, or to meet someone who can tell them more about Jesus.

THE STORY SO FAR

1 Time with God
2 The power of the Holy Spirit
3 Prayer
4 Lifestyle
5 Friendships
6 My story
7 Lead-in and lead-out, plus booklet.

Have you found your place yet? Have you got your story into shape? If you have, then ask God for the opportunity to use it in the next fortnight. Have you got a booklet that you can give away?

BOOKLETS FOR SHARING

Coming Home, Christian Publicity Organisation
How to become a follower of Jesus Christ, John Mallison, Scripture Union
Journey into Life, Norman Warren, Falcon
What's the Point? Norman Warren, Lion

S·H·A·R·I·N·G —

with a booklet

LINK: What do I believe about Jesus? (page 18)

My experience of teaching people to share their faith is that most people don't find it impossible – all they need is help to get started. I hope that you are finding this yourself. Once we get the idea, and the love of God fills us, it's really amazing what we can do.

OK. Now we've got to the point where when we talk to our friends we can tell them the story of how we came to know Jesus. Where do we go from here? The next step is to share not just our own story, but the story of what Jesus has done for them – we call this the Gospel, or the Good News. Again, many people panic, because they think that they have got to remember loads of facts – but we don't need to. There are many short booklets around that contain the facts, in an easy to read form. So why not use them to help you share Jesus? Here's how to go about it.

Preparation

Get hold of one or two leaflets which tell the story of what Jesus has done. (See the previous page for some suggestions.) Read them through and see which you find the most helpful and the easiest to read.

Now go through it a page at a time and try to see what point each page is trying to make. You need to make sure that you cover most of the following facts, and you need to know where they are in your booklet. They might not come in quite this order.

● How Jesus was born. Jesus was conceived in Mary's womb supernaturally.

● What Jesus said and did. Jesus taught about how to live to please God, how to treat others, what moral standards he expected, how and who to forgive. People were amazed at his teaching. Jesus wasn't all talk – he was a man of power: over nature, sickness, demon possession, and death. He never used his power for his own ends, nor to impress people or force them to believe.

● How Jesus lived. Jesus lived simply; he didn't have possessions or store up wealth. He trusted God to provide all that he needed. He had a great love for people, and had a deep compassion for people in trouble. He never refused his help to those who genuinely asked for it. Even his enemies

ould find nothing wrong with
his lifestyle. Jesus was tough and
uncompromising with those who
pretended to believe, who
distorted the law of God, or who
led others astray.
● How Jesus died. The death of
Jesus occupies a large amount of
the Gospels – which shows that
Jesus' crucifixion is a really
important part of the story.

Jesus' resurrection. Three days
after his death Jesus came alive
again. He was seen by Mary, by
the two disciples going to
Emmaus, by all the disciples on
various occasions, and by 500
people at once! What they saw
and experienced of the risen
Jesus convinced them that this
was the Jesus who had died and
that this was a real person not a
ghost. The disciples were
convinced. In the following 2000
years, millions have agreed with
them.
● Jesus' ascension. It was
necessary for Jesus to be taken
into heaven so that he could, by

his Spirit, be in many places. The
ascension happened at Bethany.
The disciples saw this as a joyful
moment.

Once you have got familiar with
your booklet, all you need to do
is to get to the point where
you've told your story and then
ask, 'Would you like to know
more about Jesus?' If the person
you're talking with agrees, go
through the booklet together and
give it to him or her at the end.
Don't drop them after that!
● Pray for them.
● Ask them if they've found the
booklet useful.
● Look for opportunities to take
them to another event where they
can hear about Jesus.

THE STORY SO FAR
1 Time with God
2 The power of the Holy Spirit
3 Prayer
4 Lifestyle
5 Friendships
6 My story
7 Lead-in and lead-out, plus
booklet.
8 The Gospel, using a booklet.

Have you found your place yet?
Here's a useful exercise. Get
some evangelistic booklets, pull
out the staples, get your scissors,
and get the relevant facts cut
out. This way, you'll see clearly
what it is that you need to bring
out when you talk.

Now get your tape recorder
and try recording a 'talk' to
convert yourself! It's good to
practise what you want to say,
and then to listen. I expect you'll
make a few changes after you've
done this! But it's worth the
effort.

Sharing – the facts

It's good to be able to share the facts about Jesus using a booklet. But if you can't find a booklet that's right for your friends, you could share the facts without a booklet, in a conversational way. Are you someone who could do this? Here's what you need to do.

1 Make sure you've got your story together, and have a lead-in, so that you can get started.

2 Get the facts together. You could do the scissors job suggested at the end of the previous page, or pull the facts together yourself from a Bible or a book. Here are the key ones as a reference for you, including the relevant Bible verses.

- Jesus was Mary's son (Matthew 1:18–25).
- He was God in human form (John 1:14).
- He lived a perfect life (2 Corinthians 5:21).
- He showed the way to a new sort of life – of peace, power, security, eternal life and forgiveness. We needed it because by our rebellion we had cut ourselves off from God (Romans 3:23).

- Jesus died (Mark 15).
- He came alive again (Mark 16).
- Jesus is alive today (Matthew 28:20).

3 Facts on their own don't make a lot of sense to those who don't believe in Jesus, so you've got to make the key points from the facts. Look in evangelistic leaflets to see how this is done. These are the points you've got to underline.

- God is there, and he wants a friendship with us.
- Our sin has broken that friendship.
- God's love is seen in Jesus.
- Jesus is God. He wants to restore the friendship.
- Jesus' death wasn't meaningless: it's the way to being forgiven what we've done wrong – so that we can be friends of God.
- Jesus' resurrection is proof that what he said about himself is true and reliable.
- We need to respond. (Turn over the page for more about this.)

4 To the facts and the explanations have to be added illustrations and examples from everyday life – I've already quoted a few. It's good to draw on our own daily experience of God.

5 It is important that we share these facts, explanations and illustrations in a natural and relaxed way. For example:

- we need to be friendly.
- we should talk *with* people, not *at* them. So it's okay to encourage questions, discussion, comment.
- we need to use the Bible carefully. Don't bash people with it!
- we should speak in a relaxed and normal way. We don't need to say, 'And so, as it says in John chapter three verse sixteen . . . ZAP!' Be natural and just say what it says: 'You know, Tim, God loved the world so much . . . .'

back to their objection later. My desire is to present Jesus honestly, openly and graciously. He is the answer to every objection in the end.

THE STORY SO FAR
1 Time with God
2 The power of the Holy Spirit
3 Prayer
4 Lifestyle
5 Friendships
6 My story
7 Lead-in and lead-out, plus booklet.
8 The Gospel, using a booklet or
9 The Gospel, using the facts, in a relaxed manner.

Have you found your place yet? If you're trying to learn the facts, write them out on small cards and take them with you throughout the day. Then you can practise and learn them in spare moments (like waiting for a bus). You'll soon find that you've got the hang of things and don't need the cards anymore.

Problem areas

Those who share Jesus in this way usually have a number of concerns.
• 'Am I making a fool of myself?' But does it matter? It's a joy and a privilege to share Jesus: you're no fool to do it.
• 'Do they really want to hear?' Most people are far more willing to talk about Jesus than we expect. Try it!
• 'Do they have the time to hear?' Maybe not! We shouldn't be pushy. Try asking, 'Is now an okay time to talk – or are you too busy?'
• 'Are they understanding me?' Again, maybe not. Find out by asking questions: 'Is that clear?' 'What do you think?' 'What would you have done?'
• 'Will they raise objections I can't answer?' Most people are not walking round ready to bump you with hundreds of reasons why they need not believe in Jesus. They often don't even know much about him. So don't worry about objections. I either answer them (if I can) or admit that I can't (if I can't) – and then ask them if I can come

Sharing:

Sharing the facts about Jesus, in whatever way we do it, is doing the work of an evangelist. It can, sometimes, be hard, but it brings great joy to God, and to us as well – as I hope you are finding. But there's one step more to consider – those we share with have to have the opportunity to make a response to what we have said. How are we going to give them that opportunity? How are we going to know that we've not forced them into a decision too soon nor missed an opportunity to suggest that they decide for themselves about Jesus?

3 Lead them

You can lead them in a prayer yourself, and there is no reason why you shouldn't if you feel that it is right. Follow these steps.

● Ask a few 'sorting out' questions: 'Do you understand what I've been telling you?' Give people a chance to ask questions, get things clear, and

There are three simple ways of handling responses, but before we look at them let me encourage you not to get panicky about this part of sharing your faith. We do all make mistakes, so you won't be the first, nor the last. And the Holy Spirit will lead and guide you. So relax!

1 Show them

Most leaflets contain a prayer which people can use to help them give their lives to Jesus. Point this out to your friend and

suggest that if he or she wants to follow Jesus they go away and pray that prayer. Ask them to tell you if they've done so – then you can help them in their new faith.

2 Take them

Take them to some one else who can lead them to Jesus. There might be someone in your group; or maybe an evangelistic night is being planned where there will be a chance to respond.

even say, 'I want to go away and think.' We can't force people to believe.

● Ask a 'response' question: 'Would you like to make Jesus your Saviour and Lord?' Having Jesus as Saviour means accepting that he has died to pay the price for your sins and bring you into his kingdom. Having Jesus as Lord means that he has control of your life.

–and responding

- Ask a 'making sure' question: 'Can I explain what this means?' It is important to make it clear what we are asking people to do and to give them the chance to get things clear, and to be sure about what deciding to follow Jesus means. You can explain it with an **ABC**.

It means: **A**dmit
– that in God's sight you are a wrong doer,
– that you have said and done things that are wrong.
It means: **B**elieve
– that Jesus really is God's only Son, in charge of history,
– that he loves you, and wants you to be one of his children,
– that he died for your sins and came alive again.
It means: **C**ount the cost of
– putting Jesus first in your life,
– making time for God,
– being willing to stand up for God even when things are tough.

Here is a prayer you could use. 'Dear Lord, I'm sorry for the past, for ignoring you. Please forgive me. Thank you for dying on the cross for me. I want you to be my Lord. Please come into my life right now. Help me to serve you faithfully and grow like you. Give me your Holy Spirit, to help and strengthen me.'

Common responses

When asked to make a decision about following Jesus, there are only a certain number of ways people can respond.
1 'No thanks.' If someone says this, don't be alarmed or panic. It might just as easily mean, 'Not now.' People sometimes need time to think things through. Be ready with a gracious reply and give them a leaflet to read.

2 'I've already given my life to Jesus.' This is always a good thing to hear, but don't think you have wasted your time. Sometimes people who have given their lives to Jesus have been encouraged to hear the good news again, and their faith may have been strengthened by listening to you.

3 'I'm not sure.' People who say this are often quite interested, but just need things to be made clearer. Check back over the facts with them again, to see where they are stuck.
4 'Please tell me more.' Use the various clarifying questions

above to see where they really are. Remember, this decision is between them and God, not between you and them.
5 'Yes.' Great! Helping someone become a Christian is a wonderful privilege. But what next? Don't drop them! Caring for new Christians is vital. They need:
- someone they can rely on.
- help with the Bible.
- a friend to take them to church.
- a friend they can pray with.
- a small group where they can learn and grow with others.
- help with working out how their new Christian life works.
- help with sharing Jesus with their friends.

THE STORY SO FAR
1 Time with God
2 The power of the Holy Spirit
3 Prayer
4 Lifestyle
5 Friendships
6 My story
7 Lead-in and lead-out, plus booklet.
8 The Gospel, using a booklet or
9 The Gospel, using the facts, in a relaxed manner
10 Looking for a response.
11 Caring for new Christians.

Where do you fit in? Caring for new Christians is a vital job — are you someone who can get alongside new believers, and help them for a year or so? If so, then you're very much part of the work of sharing Jesus.

Sharing –
The Problems

Sharing isn't all problems! It's so easy to think that it is, partly because we're so conscious of our own worries and partly because we think that every non-Christian is just waiting for us to open our mouths so that they can ridicule us. In my experience, while people do have genuine questions and doubts about the Christian faith they haven't thought up hundreds of reasons for not believing! Jesus is not a problem but a joy, and with this attitude in our hearts we can face anything.

So what are the problems we are likely to be facing?

Problems with you and me

1 Our own daily walk with Jesus should be in good shape. If we don't keep close to Jesus through prayer, reading the Bible and worship, then he is going to seem distant. The things we want to say will never flow easily and the enemy will try to accuse us of being lazy and undisciplined.
● Is this true for you? Stay close; and if you're not, make a new beginning today.
2 'I'm afraid.' So am I! In fact, I'm very much afraid – until I get going. We have to stand against this fear. One way to do this is to spend a little more time in the presence of Christ, telling him how much you love him and enjoying his love for you.
3 'I just don't get the chance.' When I feel like this, I go back to the Holy Spirit and ask him to fill me again and to make opportunities for me to speak about Jesus. I've never been let down yet. Within a week I've always had a chance to speak

about my faith. Go back to the Holy Spirit yourself, and ask him to make opportunities for you. He'll do it!
4 'I'm not getting anywhere.' This is another of Satan's suggestions. Of course we're getting

somewhere – we're sharing the best and most powerful message in the universe. We may not be seeing what's happening, but a lot is happening – we can be sure of it. The Bible tells us that if we resist Satan, he will go away from us. So try to put behind you the 'I'm not getting anywhere' idea!

5 'I'm afraid of making mistakes.' Welcome to the front line! I have made hundreds of mistakes as I've tried to share Jesus. It's a risky business and I often get it wrong. I don't worry too much about it – I just apologise to God and try again. It seems to me that the only alternative is to stop – and that's just what Satan wants.

Problems new Christians have

Sometimes new Christians have problems which can throw us.

1 'I don't feel any different.' We need to help new believers build their lives on the *facts* about Jesus. Help them get hold of the things in the 'What I believe about Jesus' section (page 18).

2 'I'm still sinning.' Sin separated us from God in the first place. So what happens when I sin again, having given my life to Jesus? We have to help new Christians understand these great truths.

● Nothing can separate us from God once we have become his children (see Romans 8:39).

● We can be forgiven daily (1 John 1:8–9).

3 Prayer, Bible and church problems. We must help new believers get over these problems – perhaps reading the Bible with them, praying with them or by taking them to church etc.

4 'My friends think I'm stupid.' We all know this problem don't we? Our friends ridicule us or make us look foolish. It isn't easy to stand against this kind of pressure. Have a look at what Jesus said in Mark 8:34–38.

Objections from non-Christians

As I've already said, I don't consider problems too much when I talk about Jesus. If people raise objections, I have a simple pattern which I follow.

1 I answer them, if I can. So when someone says, 'How can I know that there's a God?' I reply, 'Well, you can know him because there are three proofs of his presence – his creation, your conscience and his word, the Bible.'

2 I admit it when I can't. So when someone says, 'How can you believe in a God when there's so much suffering around,' I reply quite simply, 'I just don't know. It's really hard. But are things made any better by not believing?'

3 I offer to find an answer. If someone really wants to know something which I don't know I say, 'Look, I don't know. But I'll go and talk to someone who does, and I'll bring you back an answer. Now would you like to talk some more now, or shall we talk more when I've got an answer to your question?'

4 I do some research. I've worked out what to say to the basic objections people raise: 'How do I know if there's a God?' 'Why should I believe in your God and not Buddha?' 'I can't believe in someone I can't see!' 'I don't believe in the Bible.' You need to do the same. There are books that can give simple answers and it's good to know them.

One final word of encouragement on this subject – *be positive.*

Photographs in this book are by Gordon Gray, except those on the following pages . . .

page 3 provided by CPAS
page 6 by Adrian Meredith, © British Airways
page 9 by John Grayston
page 16 from the Imperial War Museum, © Camera Press
page 20 provided by Traidcraft
page 34 provided by Pronuptia-Youngs
page 35 by Luke Golobitsh
page 37 by Mike Webb, provided by TEAR Fund
page 40 by Jean-Luc Ray
page 42 from the Imperial War Museum
page 43 by Luke Golobitsh
page 44 provided by the Boy's Brigade
pages 46 and 47 are Crown copyright and were supplied by the Royal Marines
page 49 photograph is supplied courtesy of the Royal Mint
page 57 by Kenneth Prater, reproduced by courtesy of NCH
page 58 by Adrian Rowland, reproduced by courtesy of NCH
page 60 by Les Wilson, © Camera Press
page 61 by John Miles, provided by the press office of the General Synod of the Church of England
pages 62 and 63 are Crown copyright and are reproduced with the permission of the Controller of Her Majesty's Stationery Office
pages 64 and 65 by Angela Reith, provided by the Mildmay Mission Hospital
page 66 is the copyright of the Metropolitan Police
page 67 by Sacha Z Photography is from the cover of *Non-alcoholic cocktails* by Anne Jesper (Whittet Books Ltd)
page 69 by Dr Lennart Nilsson
page 71 by Malcolm Fielding, the BOC group PLC, from the Science Photo Library
page 77 by Nishi Sharma
page 78 by Ian Berry, supplied by Christian Aid
page 79 by Mike Goldwater, supplied by Christian Aid
page 80 supplied by kind courtesy of the Victoria and Albert Museum and Fine Art Developments

Artwork in this book is by . . .

Karen Mezek, pages 10 and 21
Taffy Davies, pages 19, 20, 30, 31, 70 and 73
Fred Apps, page 75

Credits

Cover design by Paul Edwards.
Cover photograph by Darrell Wong from Action-Plus Photographic.
Inside design by Andrew Mann.
Text on pages 35 and 73 is reproduced with permission from The Alternative Service Book 1980, copyright © The Central Board of Finance of the Church of England.

British Library Cataloguing in Publication Data

Smith, Jim, *1947–*
    Now I'm a Christian.
    1. Adolescents. Christian life
    I. Title
    248.8'3